Putting Professional Leadership into Practice in Social Work

Sara Miller McCune founded SAGE Publishing in 1965 to support the dissemination of usable knowledge and educate a global community. SAGE publishes more than 1000 journals and over 800 new books each year, spanning a wide range of subject areas. Our growing selection of library products includes archives, data, case studies and video. SAGE remains majority owned by our founder and after her lifetime will become owned by a charitable trust that secures the company's continued independence.

Los Angeles | London | New Delhi | Singapore | Washington DC | Melbourne

Putting Professional Leadership into Practice in Social Work

Peter Scourfield

SAGE | **Learning Matters**

7392

MT

Learning Matters
An imprint of SAGE Publications Ltd
1 Oliver's Yard
55 City Road
London EC1Y 1SP

SAGE Publications Inc.
2455 Teller Road
Thousand Oaks, California 91320

SAGE Publications India Pvt Ltd
B 1/I 1 Mohan Cooperative Industrial Area
Mathura Road
New Delhi 110 044

SAGE Publications Asia-Pacific Pte Ltd
3 Church Street
#10-04 Samsung Hub
Singapore 049483

Editor: Kate Keers
Development editor: Sarah Turpie
Senior project editor: Chris Marke
Project management: Deer Park Productions
Marketing manager: Camille Richmond
Cover design: Wendy Scott
Typeset by: C&M Digitals (P) Ltd, Chennai, India
Printed in the UK

Library of Congress Control Number: 2018950475

British Library Cataloguing in Publication Data

A catalogue record for this book is available from the British Library.

ISBN 978-1-5264-3002-1
ISBN 978-1-5264-3003-8 (pbk)

At SAGE we take sustainability seriously. Most of our products are printed in the UK using responsibly sourced papers and boards. When we print overseas we ensure sustainable papers are used as measured by the PREPS grading system. We undertake an annual audit to monitor our sustainability.

12/7/20

Contents

Series editor's preface

During recent teaching sessions for student social workers I have been struck keenly by the changes permeating our contemporary world. Values and ethics lie at the heart of social work, and social work education, and we address these throughout all the books in the series. The positions that we take in terms of values and ethics are, to an extent, determined by context, time and experience, these are expressed in different ways by students coming into social work education today. Since the turn of this century we have witnessed shifts and challenges as the marketised neoliberal landscape of politics, economy and social life may attract little comment or contest from some. We have observed the political machinery directing much of statutory social work towards a focus on individuals apart from their environment. However, we have also seen a new turn to the social in the #MeToo campaign where unquestioned entitlement to women's bodies and psychology is exposed and resisted. We have seen defiance of those perpetuating social injustices that see long-term migrants alongside today's migrants abused and shunned by society – institutions as well as individuals. It is likely that, as a student of social work, you will lay bare and face many previously unquestioned assumptions, which can be very perplexing and uncover needs for learning, support and understanding. This series of books acts as an aid as you make these steps. Each book stands in a long and international tradition of social work that promotes social justice and human rights, introducing you to the importance of sometimes new and difficult concepts, and inculcating the importance of close questioning of yourself as you make your journey towards becoming part of that tradition.

There are numerous contemporary challenges for the wider world, and for all four countries of the UK. These include political shifts to the 'popular' Right, a growing antipathy to care and support, and dealing with lies and 'alternative truths' in our daily lives. Alongside this, is the need to address the impact of an increasingly ageing population with its attendant social care needs, and working with the financial implications that such a changing demography brings. At the other end of the lifespan the need for high quality childcare, welfare and safeguarding services has been highlighted as society develops and responds to the changing complexion. As demand rises so do the costs, and the unquestioned assumption that austerity measures are necessary continues to create tensions and restrictions in services, policies and expectations.

It is likely that as a social worker you will work with a diverse range of people throughout your career, many of whom have experienced significant, even traumatic, events that require a professional and caring response. As well as working with individuals, however, you may be required to respond to the needs of a particular community disadvantaged by local, national or world events or groups excluded within their local communities because of assumptions made about them.

The importance of high quality social work education remains if we are adequately to address the complexities of modern life. We should continually strive for excellence in education as this allows us to focus clearly on what knowledge it is useful to engage with when learning to be a social worker. Questioning everything, especially from a position of knowledge, is central to being a social worker.

The books in this series respond to the agendas driven by changes brought about by professional bodies, governments and disciplinary reviews. They aim to build on and offer introductory texts based on up-to-date knowledge and to help communicate this in an accessible way, so preparing the ground for future study and for encouraging good practice as you develop your social work career. Each book is written by someone passionate about social work and social services and aims to instil that passion in others. In the current text Peter Scourfield introduces you to the concepts of professional leadership in beginning and continuing social work practice, setting the scene for exploring more specialised areas of practice and providing you with a grounding from which to enhance your learning. The book shows that these concepts and practices are important for good quality practice at all levels and do not simply relate to management roles or qualified practice. You will be taken through the complexities of the concepts in ways that are understandable and can be translated to your placements and early career in social work, and you will be encouraged to enhance your knowledge and skills as you progress.

Professor Jonathan Parker

August 2018

About the author

Peter Scourfield qualified as a social worker in 1984. Since then he has practised social work in a variety of settings with diverse service user groups. He has been involved full time in social work education since 2003. During this period of his career Peter has performed the roles of Course Leader on the MA Social Work programme; Practice Educator, lecturer and personal tutor on the BA Social Work, MA Social Work and Step Up to Social Work programmes. He has also been involved in Post-Qualifying social work education. His research and writing interests have mainly focused on the adult social care system. His PhD was focused on older people's experiences in the social care system. Peter is currently an Honorary Visiting Fellow at Anglia Ruskin University and a freelance writer and trainer.

Introduction

Professional leadership is a relatively new field of study within social work. This book is designed to be an introductory text which aims to make a modest but practical contribution to this growing field. A key aim of this book is to persuade people who do not necessarily regard themselves as leaders for various reasons to appreciate that, in social work, professional leadership both can and, in fact, needs to come from anyone who can provide it when the situation requires it. To this end, consider the following vignette. I am sure that it is a scenario to which most social work students can relate.

> *Chloe is in the first week of her BA Social Work course. One of the sessions is on 'qualities of a professional social worker'. The lecturer starts off by talking about the importance in social work of the concept of empathy. He insists to the group that, although similar, it is not to be confused with sympathy. After 20 minutes, the lecturer has tried hard but apparently confused the whole group with his explanation. The room is silent but there are many furrowed brows.*

We will return to this scenario at the end of this Introduction when, hopefully, the point will be made that you do not have to be a manager, supervisor or vastly experienced practitioner to perform a useful leadership role in social work. This book is primarily aimed at social work students and newly qualified social workers (NQSWs) at the Assessed and Supported Year in Employment (ASYE) and Social Worker levels of the *Professional Capabilities Framework* (PCF). That is to say the target readership is mainly those who aspire to become professional social workers and those who have just qualified and are on the first rung of their career ladder as professional social workers. You might be forgiven for thinking that, for this group, the subject of 'professional leadership' would come low on their list of priorities, if on the list at all. You might reasonably believe that, given their relative lack of experience, the main role of students and NQSWs is to follow rather than lead. You might similarly argue that professional leadership is best left to managers and to more experienced and senior colleagues – that is to say, those who are at the top of the profession and, indeed, get paid more to take the responsibility! And you might therefore assume that any thoughts of professional leadership can come later: once you have qualified, once you have acquired more knowledge and skills and once you have a few years' more experience under your belt.

These are not unreasonable thoughts to have and one would hope that students and NQSWs do continue to learn from their more experienced colleagues as their careers progress. However, current guidance governing professional social work in England – the PCF – makes it clear that all students (including those yet to start their first placement) need to demonstrate 'professional leadership'. The same applies to NQSWs and those on the 'social worker' level. As one of the domains of the PCF it is a requirement for professional qualification and it is a requirement for registration and subsequent professional progression. Therefore one important reason for writing this book is to enable you to understand this domain better and to be better able to meet the requirements for qualification. We will discuss how to do 'professional leadership' in ways that will enable you to put it into practice as a student or NQSW and either pass your qualifying course or to complete your ASYE.

For some that might suffice. However, that would be quite a narrow and instrumental way of approaching the topic. Another equally, if not more, important reason for writing the book is to explore the concept of professional leadership as it applies to social work more broadly and more critically. What makes it a particularly interesting task is that the two constituent parts that underpin the concept of professional leadership: 'professionalism' and 'leadership' are both open to a variety of interpretations, ideas and theories. When applied to social work – itself a hugely contested subject – it makes the challenge of defining what constitutes professional leadership and thinking about how it can be put into practice all the more exciting to explore.

The book is structured in such a way as to enable you to explore each of these key concepts in more depth before moving on to looking more specifically at what professional leadership might mean and look like in everyday practice. The various discussions and exercises should enable you to see that all of us involved in social work, whatever our role, share collective responsibility for professional leadership. This would be from first year students in their first class at university through to frontline practitioners, supervisors, line managers, practice educators, all the way to those at very top of the profession. We might not all practise professional leadership in the same way or have the opportunities to practise it all of the time. For many of us we will spend as much time, if not more, following rather than leading. Nevertheless, the fact that when the occasion demands it we are able and willing to take a lead is an integral part of ensuring that the profession of social work remains fit for purpose, keeps to its core values, is safe, has the confidence of the public and other professionals and continues to develop to meet the many challenges created by today's fast changing world.

Chapter 1 is all about unpicking concepts relating to professions and professionalism generally. It begins by discussing ideas about what it means to call someone or something 'professional'. It then examines the concept of professionalism and contrasts this with the less well-known concept of 'professionality', before exploring how professionalism might be defined in terms of professional competencies. We discuss different ideas about what constitutes a profession. This leads us onto thinking about the power and status of professions and what role professions play in society. This chapter aims to create a context in which we can think more critically about social work as a profession and what it means to be a social work professional.

In Chapter 2 we look at how, over the last century or so, the status of social work has gradually changed from a fragmented and diverse set of welfare activities, mainly carried out by well-meaning amateurs, to the 'profession' it is today. This discussion will not only focus on the processes of professionalisation that took place over the course of the twentieth century but also the so-called 'deprofessionalisation' and 'reprofessionalisation' of social work that have taken place in recent decades. We will consider claims that there is still considerable debate today, not only about whether social work status is a profession, but also whether it *should* be a profession. Given the many social, political and demographic factors as well as policy directives that impact on social work, we discuss the challenges facing the social work profession in contemporary society. This will involve examining key messages from recent reports and policy aimed at social work. In doing so this will explain the background to why professional leadership has become embedded in discourses on social work to the point that it is now a domain in its own right in the current PCF and signalled in newly created roles such as those of Chief Social Worker and Principal Social Worker.

Chapter 3 explores the concept of leadership generally. This is because, as Northouse (2015a, p. 8) makes clear, 'how you think about leadership will strongly influence how you practice leadership'. The first part looks more closely at definitions of leadership, ideas about what leaders do, different leadership roles and capabilities. There are a vast number of theories of and models of leadership in circulation and, in order to select an appropriate model for social work, we focus on the idea of the 'incomplete leader' as developed by Ancona et al. (2007), who argue the merits of a collective or 'distributed' model of leadership. This seems to be a model of leadership implied in much social work policy and practice guidance.

Ancona et al. view leadership as essentially encompassing four main capabilities: sense-making, relating, visioning and inventing, in which no single person can excel, hence the need for everyone to take responsibility when the occasion demands it. For this reason, we also discuss how situational models of leadership are relevant in understanding how professional leadership can be practised in social work. The second part of the chapter looks at the emerging topic of 'followership' and explores various ideas about the different relationships between leaders and followers.

Chapter 4 focuses more specifically on understanding leadership in the context of social work. It seeks to explore factors in the different contexts in which social work takes place that can either limit or enable the possibilities of professional leadership being practised effectively. More specifically, we discuss factors about organisations that can influence the potential for effective professional leadership. In this respect we examine the potentially positive impact that professional networks and communities of practice can make on professional leadership.

Chapter 5 focuses on how social workers and social work students can put professional leadership into practice. We return to the concept of the 'incomplete leader' to understand better how core capabilities outlined by Ancona et al. such as sense-making, visioning and leadership might be practised in social work. The chapter then turns more specifically to examine how professional leadership is conceptualised in professional social work guidance. In this regard we reflect on the part professional leadership can play in professional socialisation and discuss the importance of role-modelling and formal and informal supervision in this process. Throughout, the chapter encourages you to reflect critically on the skills, qualities and knowledge required by leaders and followers in putting professional leadership into practice.

Chapter 6 aims to draw together various key points from the preceding chapters. It begins by encouraging reflection upon the bigger ('macro') leadership challenges facing social work. This emphasises the importance of understanding the contexts in which any such challenges arise. The chapter then focuses more on the smaller 'micro' challenges of professional leadership by suggesting leadership activities and opportunities appropriate for social work students at different stages, NQSWs and social workers generally.

Throughout the book there are illustrative case studies and a range of interactive activities that enable students to understand the knowledge and skills required in practising professional leadership in real-life contexts. Each chapter ends with a summary of its key points and suggestions for further reading.

Finally, to conclude this introduction, let us return to Chloe in her first week on her social work course.

> *'Right, if that's all OK we can move on. Any questions?' the lecturer asks. A nervous silence settles over the group. Chloe clears her throat: 'Er, yes; it might just be me being thick, but I don't think I really got it. Can you give us some examples that show the differences between the two?' The group breathes a collective sigh of relief. Someone has taken the lead and articulated their confusion. Prompted by this contribution from Chloe, the lecturer apologies for not explaining it very well and, after more explanation and more questions, the group understand better. After the session several of her classmates come up to Chloe and thank her for breaking the silence. Many wanted to ask a question but were either too anxious or didn't want to show their ignorance in front of others. Thanks to Chloe's actions, not only her classmates but also the lecturer were off on a sounder footing as they explored key professional social work concepts.*

Had not Chloe shown a form of leadership that had contributed to her own professional development and that of others?

1: What Do We Mean by Professional and Professionalism?

Achieving a social work degree

This chapter will enable you to develop the following capabilities to the appropriate level from the PCF:

- professional leadership
- professionalism.

It will also introduce you to the following academic standards as set out in the social work subject benchmark statement:

5. 3   Values and ethics
5.17   Skills in personal and professional development

More specifically it will enable you to:

- explore ideas about what makes something or someone 'professional';
- reflect critically upon concepts of professionalism;
- examine ideas about what defines a profession.

Introduction

A basic assumption underpinning this book is that how we approach professional leadership in social work will be bound up with our ideas and beliefs about critical questions that relate not only to social work but also to professions and professionalism generally. Because the focus is professional leadership in social work, clearly we need to think about what leadership means and what it requires, but, equally importantly, we also need to engage with questions about the purpose, tasks and values of social work and what constitutes professional practice in social work. However, these questions are inevitably linked to broader questions about what defines professionalism and what we expect of professionals. Underlying both these sets of questions are, perhaps, even more fundamental questions of whether social work is, can be or should actually be regarded as a profession and, assuming that it is, what type of profession it is and aspires to be. These questions have been part of social work discourse and debated keenly for many decades. They cannot be easily resolved and they will not be resolved in this book. However, neither can they be glossed over. They need careful consideration if professional leadership in social work is going to be a meaningful activity.

You might well say that the questions posed above are substantially dealt with and answered in professional codes and frameworks laid down by social work's professional and regulatory bodies. After all, social work in England is based upon a *Professional capabilities framework* (PCF) (BASW, 2018b), is an occupation regulated by the Health and Care Professions Council (HCPC) and has a professional association – BASW (the British Association of Social Workers). However, while official codes and frameworks lay down the goals of what social work is meant to achieve and also what professional qualities and behaviour are expected of social workers in meeting these goals, how these codes and expectations are interpreted and enacted in practice in specific everyday situations inevitably varies from practitioner to practitioner, from team to team and from organisation to organisation. While there will be broad agreement, there will also be differences in interpretation about what constitutes professionalism.

Given the nature, range and complexity of the work in which social workers are involved, it is not surprising that views differ about what professional social work is generally and also what constitutes professional practice in any particular situation. This is made all the more challenging because the various contexts in which social work takes place are constantly changing. Therefore, for social workers, social work students, social work educators and others involved in social work, making sense of and defining what constitutes professionalism in social work is an ongoing project that is never complete. As will be argued in subsequent chapters, an important function of professional leadership is making sense of what constitutes professionalism in social work and how it should be put into practice, both in general and in specific situations. Because of the wide ranging nature of the task, everyone involved in social work can and needs to play their part in this process.

In this chapter we start by exploring the various meanings attached to terms like 'professional' and 'professionalism', which circulate both in lay and professional discourses. Activities will encourage you to reflect upon the various ways in which we use these terms and how meanings change depending on a range of factors. You will be prompted to think about whether it is possible to identify the basic ingredients of professionalism and come to a shared understanding of what we expect from a professional, whatever occupational activity they may be undertaking.

We discuss the concept of 'professionality' as a way of understanding professionalism both in terms of the behaviour of an occupational group as a whole and in terms of the behaviour of individual practitioners in that group.

Lastly, we look at the defining characteristics of a profession in the traditional or 'classic' sense of the word. This will enable us to start thinking more critically about social work's status as a profession. This will also link us directly with Chapter 2, where we will examine in more detail how diverse forms of 'social work' activity in the nineteenth century gradually developed into the 'professional' occupation it is considered to be today.

What does it mean to call someone or something 'professional'?

In all walks of life, to call someone or something 'professional' seems to make it special in some way. For example, the phrase 'in my professional opinion' seems to carry more weight than simply 'in my opinion'. If a friend decorates our bathroom and we are pleased with it we might compliment them not just by telling them that they have done a 'good job' but that they have done a 'professional job'. There are a very large number of such examples that could be used from all sorts of contexts. In the field of social work, appeals to social workers' 'professional' selves are diverse and many. In matters of safeguarding, for example, social workers are increasingly exhorted to exercise their 'professional' judgement. The publication of an official report, such as a serious case review, might remind social workers of their 'professional' duties and responsibilities. Social workers are also expected to respect 'professional' boundaries, attend to their continuing 'professional' development and abide by 'professional' codes of ethics. It is not uncommon to hear that social workers need to develop their 'professional' identity. It is interesting to consider how the addition of 'professional' in those sentences changes their meaning, if at all. For example, what is the difference between using 'judgement' and 'professional judgement'? What actually is a 'professional' boundary, who decides where it should be erected and around what exactly? Why is it important to develop a 'professional' identity in order to do your job properly? In what ways are the normal contractual responsibilities that come with doing a paid job different from 'professional' responsibilities?

So, while there is no doubt that, when used in certain contexts, the use of 'professional' as a qualifying adjective can alter meaning, the question is in what ways and to what effect? We know that professionals cannot always agree the answers to these questions among themselves. We also know that those who use professional services can hold different opinions again about what they consider is professional and what is not. Against this background of potential conceptual and terminological confusion, it is therefore useful to begin to explore this concept in more depth, with the goal of finding common ground but also identifying possible areas of ambiguity and differences in meaning.

Activity 1.1   What is 'professional'? Definitions and synonyms

The Oxford Dictionary Online contains the following definition:

Definitions

Professional

Adjective

1 Relating to or belonging to a profession.

'young professional people'

1.1 Worthy of or appropriate to a professional person; competent, skilful, or assured.

'his professional expertise'

'their music is both memorable and professional'

2 Engaged in a specified activity as one's main paid occupation rather than as an amateur.

'a professional boxer'

2.1 *derogatory, informal* Habitually making a feature of a particular activity or attribute.
'a professional gloom-monger'

Noun

1 A person engaged or qualified in a profession.

'professionals such as lawyers and surveyors'

1.1 A person engaged in a specified activity, especially a sport, as a main paid occupation rather than as a pastime.

'his first season as a professional'

1.2 A person competent or skilled in a particular activity.

'she was a real professional on stage'

https://en.oxforddictionaries.com/definition/professional

Synonyms

An online thesaurus (http://www.thesaurus.com/browse/professional) provides the following synonyms for 'professional':

Adj. skilled, trained

- competent
- efficient
- experienced
- licensed
- qualified
- skilful
- ace
- adept
- crackerjack
- expert
- sharp
- slick
- there
- able
- acknowledged
- finished
- knowing one's stuff
- known
- learned
- on the ball
- polished
- practised
- proficient
- up to speed
- well-qualified

Questions

Read through both the definitions and synonyms provided.

1. Which definitions or synonyms best capture your own ideas about what professional means?
2. Which definitions or synonyms would you not include yourself?
3. Are there any definitions, synonyms or qualities that you feel have been omitted and need to be included?
4. If you had to define professional in just one sentence, what would it be?
5. What are your reflections on this exercise? Has it made deciding what is 'professional' in any given context easier or more difficult?
6. Share your thoughts with another.

Commentary

You have been presented with a variety of definitions and synonyms relating to 'professional'. Arguably, at least three broad themes are detectable in the lists provided. There were also some noticeable omissions. The three broad themes are as follows.

Expert/competent

The first theme is that we usually regard a 'professional' as someone who has a recognisable level of expertise or competence in a specific area and whose work is regarded as achieving a certain standard or quality.

Paid

Second, in everyday usage, being 'a professional' often refers to the fact that someone is paid for what they do and usually they make their main livelihood from a particular activity or occupation.

Trained

Third, in the definitions and synonyms provided there are indications that 'professional' is associated with ideas about being specially 'qualified', 'trained' or 'certified' in some way.

Finally, it is worth making the point that even within these broad headings, there could be differences of opinion on a range of matters – for example, what exactly the 'professional' standard is for any piece of work and what counts as the proper level of training.

Omissions

While the three themes above were evident, there were some interesting omissions. For example, in some contexts, we talk about the concepts of 'professional discretion', 'professional autonomy' and 'professional authority'. This implies that it is the mark of a professional that their expertise is such that we place our trust in them to make the correct judgement call or do the right thing in certain situations. This puts professionals in a powerful position of authority. Indeed, many are inclined to mistrust professionals for this very reason. The issues of professional power, authority and trust, in turn, raise questions of both 'professional ethics' and 'professional accountability' – that is to say, to whom are professionals answerable and against which or whose standards of conduct? Interestingly, you might have flagged up that terms such as 'powerful', 'trustworthy', 'ethical' and 'accountable' were absent from the lists provided and these are important dimensions of being professional to which we will need to return to later.

This exercise illustrates that, whether used as a noun or an adjective, 'professional' has several meanings and that an important factor that shapes meaning is the particular context in which the term is used. The list of synonyms is interesting because it underlines the variety of associations that 'professional' has in everyday discourse. Again, context is important in this respect, as is the perspective of those concerned.

Professionalism

Like 'professional', 'professionalism' is a concept that has meanings that shift in different contexts. A standard dictionary definition states that professionalism is: 'the competence or skill expected of a professional' (https://en.oxforddictionaries.com/definition/professionalism).

On its own this definition will not get us very far. However, following on from the previous discussion, we could elaborate and say that professionalism encompasses the entirety of the mindset, skillset, values, competence, experience and training expected of professionals, as well as their orientation towards society in general.

Professionalism and professionality

When we talk about 'professionalism' it can refer to the practices of an individual practitioner but also to the practices of the profession as whole. So, for example, we might hear that, following a terrorist incident, a certain police officer 'acted with great professionalism'. Equally, we might hear it said that 'the Metropolitan Police needs to be commended for its professionalism in the way that it has dealt with the terrorist threat in recent years'. In the latter case, it would not be a comment on every single officer's behaviour (this is bound to fluctuate between individuals); it would more be a comment about the overall operations, culture and leadership of the organisation as a whole. This is a subtle but important distinction to make in how we use the term.

To avoid conceptual and terminological confusion some draw a distinction between 'professionalism' and 'professionality', believing that 'professionalism' best describes the culture and practices of the professional group as a whole, whereas 'professionality' refers to how individual practitioners interpret the broader professional culture, professional values and standards in their own practice. For example, Evans (2008, p. 8) defines professionality as: 'an ideologically-, attitudinally-, intellectually-, and epistemologically-based stance on the part of an individual, in relation to the practice of the profession to which s/he belongs, and which influences her/his professional practice'.

Therefore, while we might talk about how, say, a profession should improve its *professionalism*, one would talk about the need for an individual practitioner to work on their *professionality*. While this is a very useful terminological and conceptual distinction to make, the problem is that few people within, and even fewer outside, professions make this distinction and 'professionality' is a term seldom used in this way. There is, for example, no reference to 'professionality' in the PCF for qualified social workers and social work students in England (BASW, 2018b). The terminology used throughout is 'professionalism'. However, it seems obvious that its use encompasses both the 'professionalism' (of the profession) and the 'professionality' (of the individual practitioner). Mainly because the term 'professionality' is not commonly used in professional social work discourse (if at all), the term will not be used here. However, it is a useful distinction that is made by Evans and needs to be borne in mind.

Finally, while it is interesting to discuss professionalism in the abstract, it is essential that we examine professionalism made 'concrete' – that is to say, when it is translated into behaviour, enacted in practice and has an impact on people's lives. Therefore, we need to consider professionalism in terms of how professionals actually are (individually and collectively), what they do, how they perform their role and the impact that they have, day by day and week by week.

Professionalism and professional competence

While the PCF sets out the standards of professionalism for qualified social workers and social work students in England, it would be fair to say that service users, carers, other professionals and members of the public in general will almost certainly *not* use the PCF to make *their* judgements about a particular social work department's or social worker's professionalism.

Case study 1.1   Roy

Roy is living with dementia. His deteriorating cognitive abilities mean that his capacity to live independently looks increasingly risky. Although Roy is happy as he is, his daughters (Maria and Tanya) asked their local adult social care team to visit to assess him. Both daughters were present at the assessment. Maria showed the social worker evidence of Roy's failing mental powers and the risks to health and safety that these created – for example, where Roy had recently burned out a saucepan on the gas hob. At the end, the social worker said that he could see that there were certain risks that needed to be managed. However, he would need to make another visit because, on the evidence of that meeting alone, he could not clearly establish whether Roy had the capacity to make decisions about his own living arrangements.

The sisters disagreed about the social worker's professionalism. Tanya liked his 'bedside manner' and the way he wanted to get to know Roy as an individual. He spent time asking Roy about his past life, how long he had lived in the house and what his interests were. Tanya thought that the social worker behaved like someone who their father would trust to do the 'professional' thing.

Maria was frustrated that the social worker insisted on trying to engage Roy in what she described as 'mainly irrelevant chitchat'. Maria did not think that the social worker recognised the seriousness of the risks of Roy staying at home and the fact that he urgently needed to move to a safer environment. He had failed to listen properly to the evidence provided by the people who knew Roy best – his daughters. Maria felt that, as a professional, the social worker needed to have been less 'dithery' and more decisive.

As case study 1.1 indicates everybody has their own ideas about what professionalism means and looks like in particular contexts. That is why it is useful to explore as many ideas about professionalism as possible, rather than just focus on those provided by the professions themselves. Therefore, at this stage, it is useful to reflect upon professionalism in ways that consumers, ordinary members of the public and other professionals might conceive of it. This will enable us to see whether it is possible to identify basic principles or ingredients of professionalism that would apply, whatever service or occupational group is concerned.

At different points in our lives we will all need to use or call upon the 'professional' services of a range of occupations. These might include: doctors, lawyers, dentists, accountants, architects, engineers, mechanics, IT specialists, builders, pharmacists, teachers, nurses and social workers. We usually do so with some expectations about what quality of service we expect and the behaviour of those involved. The activity below requires you to think about what basic standards and qualities of professionalism you would expect from a professional, whatever service they were providing.

Activity 1.2

In pairs discuss:

- When you use a professional service, what are your expectations about the standard of service/quality of work you will receive?
- What knowledge, skills and competences and other qualities do you expect the professionals delivering that service to possess?
- What would you do, or what would you expect to happen, if you considered that professional standards had not been met?
- Share your thoughts with another pair.

Commentary

Standard of service

In answer to the first question you might have discussed how, when we use or engage a professional service, the very least we expect is that the standard of their work fulfils the remit, meets the requirements of the job in hand and is fit for purpose. It needs to meet the 'industry standard' in the sense that if another independent person from the same profession was brought in they would judge the quality to be at least satisfactory, even if they might do it differently.

Knowledge, skills and competences

For question two you might have discussed that a professional's knowledge and skills also have to be fit for purpose, so that they can demonstrate expertise in the area in which they are practising. This would mean that both knowledge and skills were relevant and up to date. Your views might have differed on the specific service you had in mind; however, it is likely that, whatever the job, most people would expect professionalism to involve being well-organised, skilled in communication, approachable, trustworthy and reliable, while wanting to do the best job possible and paying attention to detail.

Other qualities

The professionalism that some people look for begins and ends with the level of competence that the professional brings to the job. Yet, for some of us, that might be missing an important ingredient of what we look for in professionalism – that is, to work ethically and to be guided by higher ideals than simply self-interest. For some, a hallmark of professionalism is that the motivation to work for the benefit of others takes precedence over the motivation to make money. For example, when clients pay for their service professionalism means advising the client of the best value options rather than what would be most profitable for the professional and their business. It is important to consider the importance of ethics because, as was proposed earlier, with knowledge and expertise comes power (Johnson, 1972; Parker and Doel, 2013) and we need to be confident that professionals do not abuse their power. This links to the question of what can be done if a professional service falls below the standard we expect. What powers of redress do *we* have?

Standard not met

Your responses probably differed depending on what type of professional service was involved. In cases that involved payment, if the professional did not complete the work to your satisfaction, you might demand your money back, possibly even threatening legal action. However, not all professional transactions involve payment. In these cases you might first request a second opinion and/or you might want to make a formal complaint. If it was a health professional, the poor practice might be such that you were worried about the treatment of people other than yourself, for example. This raises the question of where you would direct your complaint. Some professional occupations have more formal procedures than others and are covered by different regulatory regimes. With some of the more traditional professions such as law and medicine, the profession makes its own rules and oversees itself. For others, an independent regulatory body decides what the professional standards are for that occupation. However, professionals like lawyers and doctors do not always work independently and things change if such a professional is employed in a public organisation. In some cases, professionals are answerable to their professional body, their employing organisation, as well as being answerable in law. Therefore, different codes and rules apply to different occupational groups in different situations. It is not always easy for 'consumers' of professional services to know what their rights are and to know what is available to them when standards are not met. It is not difficult to see how imbalances of power can arise.

In Chapter 2 we will look at how the importance of gathering the perspectives of service users has only relatively recently become recognised in social work, but is now considered to be an essential standard by which professional social work is evaluated.

Perspectives on professionalism and professional competence

Different academics and occupational groups have long endeavoured to provide their own definitions of what professionalism means (Johnson, 1972; Blackmore, 1999). An internet search will soon show that this endeavour continues for many groups. For example, see this recent attempt by the Florida Bar Standing Committee on Professionalism:

http://www.smartbizlaw.com/Professionalism-Expectations-FINAL-ADA.pdf

Two more such attempts are provided for you to read from the following sources.

One

In 1985 a panel involving occupations ranging from business administration, engineering to aerospace was asked to say what they believed the 'ingredients of professionalism' were. They, naturally, came to the discussion from a variety of angles. The moderator proposed that important aspects of professionalism to be discussed were: responsibility; special training; altruism; effective communication; competence; ethical conduct; and respect for self and others. A computer scientist contributed:

> We expect the professional not only to do specialized and skilful work, but to take pride in their work, to be internally driven to do a good job technically and socially. We expect the professional to consider all aspects of the issue as a package, so that appropriate actions are taken. We expect the professional to hold himself accountable for his actions.

Another contributor said:

> I believe the two most important ingredients for professionalism are ethics and competence. A professional must always be honest and impartial; willing to discuss any (potential) conflicts; aware of society's and other parties' interests, as well as those of the clients; must deliver the "correct" answer to the problem (not just what the client wants); charge a fair price; etc.

Another made these points:

> Professionals share two very obvious characteristics. They are (1) a recognized and well publicized code of ethics and (2) some form of certification.
>
> Even before examining the requirements of a profession, however, we may wish to give a good deal of thought to the desirability of being 'professionals' at all. **Do we want or need this label?** {my bold}

> Ingredients of professionalism: A panel discussion, https://classes.soe.ucsc.edu/cmpe080e/Spring07/ingredients_of_professionalism.pdf

Two

Epstein and Hundert (2002, p. 226) focused on the training of physicians in medical schools. With the purpose of being able to assess and evaluate the standards of professionalism of doctors, Epstein and Hundert defined 'professional competence' as: 'the habitual and judicious use of communication, knowledge, technical skills, clinical reasoning, emotions, values, and reflection in daily practice for the benefit of the individual and community being served'. They set out seven 'dimensions of professional competence'. While some of the dimensions are more specific to medical practice, four would be applicable to most professions. They are as follows:

Cognitive

The 'cognitive' domain requires core knowledge such as basic communication skills; information management; applying knowledge to real-world situations; using tacit knowledge and personal experience; abstract problem-solving; self-directed acquisition of new knowledge; recognising gaps in knowledge; generating questions; using resources (e.g. published evidence, colleagues) and learning from experience.

Relationship

The 'relationship' domain requires communication skills; skills in handling conflict, teamwork and teaching others (e.g. patients, students and colleagues).

Affective/moral

The affective/moral domain requires the ability to tolerate ambiguity and anxiety; emotional intelligence; respect for patients; responsiveness to patients and society; and caring (p. 226).

Habits of mind

Finally, Epstein and Hundert highlight the importance of 'habits of mind'. These involve observations of one's own thinking, emotions and techniques; attentiveness, critical curiosity; recognition of and response to cognitive and emotional biases; and a willingness to acknowledge and correct errors.

Activity 1.3

1. In the previous activity you provided your own views on professionalism. After reading the extracts above, what are your issues of agreement and disagreement with the points made? Give reasons.
2. What are your thoughts about the 'affective/moral' and 'habits of mind' domains put forward by Epstein and Hundert generally, but also in respect of social work?
3. What are your thoughts about the final sentence from the first source generally, but also in respect of social work?

Commentary

Having been invited to think about your own views on professionalism and then been presented with the views of others, hopefully it was possible to identify some points in common. Some aspects of professionalism are obviously going to be specific to a particular occupation – for example, the possession of certain technical skills. However, arguably, there are generic aspects of professionalism that would be applicable in any context – for example, good communication skills, impartiality and ethical behaviour. Nevertheless, different people are bound to emphasise different qualities and skills and have their own ideas and priorities depending on their particular values and standpoint generally.

Epstein and Hundert make several interesting points. For example, they highlight that an important dimension of professional competence is the ability to look at, monitor and manage one's self. This applies as much to the affective/moral domain (recognising and managing our emotions) as it does to the cognitive domain (keeping up to date with knowledge and skills). Earlier, we talked briefly about the notion of 'professional' boundaries and, arguably, the emotional intelligence that Epstein and Hundert highlight is helpful in this respect (see, for example, *Community Care*, 2017a). It helps the professional to be attentive and caring without getting over involved personally, with the attendant loss of objectivity and the risk of one's judgement becoming clouded. The ability to develop professional 'habits of mind' is clearly an important part of monitoring one's own thinking and feelings. This relates strongly to the practice of reflexivity and critical reflection in social work (Knott and Scragg, 2016). It recognises that, in many respects, the professional's own self is, perhaps, their most important tool of trade.

Why any particular occupational group would want or need to call itself 'professional' is a really good question to consider. It is particularly relevant to social work. It not only takes us back to what we think professional and professionalism mean, but it also signals that we should be thinking more critically about what a profession actually is and what purpose professions have in society. If we relate this to social work we could ask not only *what* is gained by social work being a profession but also *who* gains and in what ways?

In *What is professional social work?* the respected social work academic Malcolm Payne asks whether social work is 'a profession or is it "just" a job?' (Payne, 2006, p. 143). In doing so, Payne not only highlights the historic and ongoing uncertainty about the status of social work as an occupational activity. He also raises more basic questions about what is special about a profession – as opposed, say, to a trade, a craft or any occupation. As stated earlier, in the eyes of its own official regulatory and professional bodies, social work is now a profession, but, as will be apparent throughout the book, what this means continues to be a matter of debate. We will continue to engage with these questions in subsequent chapters, but it should be reiterated now that an important challenge for professional leadership in social work is to engage with questions about what type of profession social work is and should be; what the roles and tasks of professional social work are; and what being a professional social worker means in practice.

Overall, these initial sections and activities underline that the concepts of 'professional' and 'professionalism' are not fixed, universally agreed entities. They are socially constructed and, as such, they are negotiable, contestable and subject to change according to a range of factors, including the specific context in which they develop and the perspective of those involved (Evetts, 2003). If we accept the constructed nature of these concepts, we can then consider the parts played by different actors in the process of construction. We can also consider what their goals and motives might be and also what impact this has on those both inside and outside of the 'profession'.

What is a profession?

The previous two sections have illustrated that, although they are at least semantically rooted in the concept of a 'profession', the terms 'professional' and 'professionalism' have taken on their own meanings in different contexts. The relationship between the three concepts is not as tight as one might expect. So, for example, someone can be considered to have done a 'professional' (i.e. competent) job without necessarily being a member of a profession. Someone can show professionalism even though, strictly speaking, they are not a 'professional' and so on. As Pierson (2011, p. 207) says, being professional is one thing, but being part of a 'recognized profession is something quite different'. This suggests that membership of a profession not only carries with it a special status, but also yet more elevated expectations of what constitutes professional behaviour and professionalism than might be applied in other occupations. In later chapters we will engage with questions about what the 'professional' means in 'professional leadership'. However, first we examine ideas about what actually defines a profession.

In medieval times there were only three 'professions': the church, the law and medicine. Despite the fact that many other occupations have attained some form of professional status in more recent years, many students of the professions still believe these foundational professions provide the benchmarks against which other occupations should be measured (for a good summary of different sides to this argument, see Evetts, 2003). However, given that social work's status as a 'profession' has been such a matter of debate for so long, we should at least conclude the chapter by examining ideas about what actually defines or constitutes a profession and also consider how and why professions come into being. This will prove a useful foundation for when we move on to consider the development of social work as an occupation in Chapter 2.

Much has been written about the status of professions and many have attempted to delineate the defining characteristics of a profession. Two broad approaches have emerged:

one that focuses on the traits or characteristics that differentiate certain professions from other (non-professional) occupations and one that focuses on the roles or functions that professions play in society. Etzioni, 1969; Johnson, 1972; Abbott, 1988; and Crompton, 1990 have made important contributions in this field and are listed in the suggestions for further reading. However, two definitions taken from the social work literature provide useful summaries that combine elements of both the trait and functional approaches.

Activity 1.4   Definitions and characteristics of professions

Definition one

Profession: a group or body, of some social standing, claiming expertise in an area of work. Features thought to characterise a profession include lengthy training in relation to some clearly demarcated area of knowledge and skill, the idea of public service or even altruistic practice, impartial service regardless of client, uniform (that is, competent) service regardless of practitioner, and a code of ethics or conduct. The classic concept of the profession, based on the medical and legal professions in the nineteenth century included a scale of fees and a commitment to independence, the latter implying that none could possibly judge the individual professional except a peer or colleague (Pierson and Thomas, 2002, p. 375).

Definition two

Profession: An occupation that has traditionally been regarded as having a number of characteristics: a code of ethics/conduct; a regulatory body; a knowledge base; and control over new entrants. There has been debate about the extent to which social work possesses these characteristics, leading some to argue that it should be regarded as, at least, a semi-profession (Harris and White, 2013, p. 366).

To reflect upon and discuss

In pairs or small groups:

1. From the two extracts provided, what are proposed as the defining characteristics of a profession?
2. What are your reflections about how a profession has been defined by both sets of authors?
3. From your knowledge of social work, why might Harris and White state that 'there has been debate about the extent to which social work possesses these characteristics'?

Commentary

Knowledge base/(lengthy) training period

Both sets of authors agree that for an occupational group to be described as a 'profession' it needs to have 'a clearly demarcated area of knowledge and skill' or 'knowledge base', although this prompts further questions, such as what is meant by the knowledge base being 'clearly demarcated' and who demarcates it? With some professions – for example, medicine and nursing – much of the knowledge base is shared. Also, in the digital world much more knowledge is more widely available to more people, so this potentially makes claims to exclusive knowledge more difficult. Pierson and Thomas also make the point that this acquisition of knowledge would include a lengthy training period. This raises questions of what the 'lengthy training period' consists of and who decides what the content should be – for example, the profession itself or some other body?

Code of ethics or conduct

Both definitions agree that a profession requires a code of 'ethics or conduct'. This appears to be an area where some occupations which regard themselves as 'professions' do not meet this particular criterion. On the one hand, an example that readily springs to mind is the music profession, where there might well be debates about what constitutes ethical behaviour but there is no binding, formal code of conduct as such. On the other hand, some areas of business that would not normally be considered professions as such do have codes of conduct based upon ethical principles (like McDonald's, for example). This highlights that the existence of a code of conduct in itself need not be the sign of a profession. We should be curious as to the principles upon which any such codes are based.

Implied in the idea of having a code of ethics or conduct is not only the belief that the public can have trust in the integrity of the profession but also that something consequential might happen if a member of the profession breaches the code. Pierson (2011, p. 61) states that a 'quintessential badge of a profession is establishing a register for qualified practitioners from which they could be struck off'. However, again, this raises questions about not only who draws up the code and on what basis, but also what happens in cases where the code is breached and how this is decided.

Public/altruistic service

Pierson and Thomas talk about a profession being founded on the idea of public or altruistic service. Altruism means the disinterested and selfless concern for the well-being of others. This characteristic basically means that professions operate on the principle of putting the interests of the public over those of their members. This is a principle that has been put to the test many times, with perhaps the most well-known example being the initial opposition of the medical profession to the creation of the National Health Service in the 1940s (Midwinter, 1994). This potential point of conflict comes to the fore just about every time doctors and other professionals such as teachers vote to go on strike. The defence put forward by professionals that, by sticking to their professional principles and looking after their own interests, the public is served better is not uncommon but contentious. Several other pertinent questions could be raised on this topic. For example, who decides what constitutes altruistic practice, how is this monitored and enforced and what happens to a professional if their practice is not always altruistic? These questions link to ideas about professional independence, autonomy and accountability.

Independence (autonomy)

Pierson and Thomas also refer to how the 'classic concept' of the profession includes 'a commitment to independence', meaning that the profession in question is left alone to judge the professional behaviour and standards of its members (Pierson and Thomas 2002: 357). Therefore, in the traditional sense, a profession is ultimately only accountable to itself. This is often referred to as professional autonomy. A profession's independence can be manifested in other ways. For example, if it is possible to make one's living solely from private practice, as is the case with the law and medicine, then such financial independence further strengthens professional autonomy. Harris and White also highlight the fact that, traditionally, a profession has 'control over new entrants' (Harris and White 2013: 366). Therefore, historically, control over the professional knowledge base and necessary skills required, control over entry to the profession, professional self-regulation and the potential for financial independence from private practice were once key characteristics of the older established professions. However, this is not necessarily the case now for these professions and, clearly, this is not the case for the many newer professions that have emerged in the last century or so. Nevertheless, this does not make issues relating to a profession's independence and autonomy any less vital to consider.

Other points of interest; status, power and the relationship with the state

Two other noteworthy points emerge in the first sentence of the definition provided by Pierson and Thomas. They explain that a profession is 'a group or body, of some *social standing*, *claiming* expertise in an area of work' {my italics} (Pierson and Thomas 2002: 416). The point about the group's 'social standing' can have different shades of meaning. For example, it could mean that a group having special expertise in an area of knowledge that is highly valued socially or economically enhances its social standing (e.g. medicine), or that the group's existing social standing enables it to make claims of expertise (e.g. the church). For most professions it is possibly a combination of both as the profession develops. Whether and why professions enjoy greater social status and, if so, how this might affect them and those they serve are interesting questions to think about. For example, if a profession has a special standing in society, arguably, it increases its power and influence but does it also mean that its behaviour comes under additional scrutiny with higher standards of behaviour expected? As far as this relates to social work, it is well known that social workers have seldom enjoyed any great standing in society. If anything, they are periodically the targets for public vilification. If the answer to Payne's question was that social work is 'just a job' then maybe it would not get such a hard time from certain quarters. Whether acquiring profession status has affected social work's social standing in any way, and what the effects of this are, is difficult to assess but is another important point to think about.

The choice of the phrase 'claiming expertise' could imply that, in advancing its own claims to special knowledge and skills, a profession not only seeks to be treated as an authority in a specific area, but also that, in doing so, it – either consciously or unconsciously – downgrades the knowledge claims of others outside of the profession. We see this at work in the debates between conventional and alternative medicine, for example. Again, the relationships between professional knowledge, professional autonomy, economic and social power become apparent.

In a later passage in their definition Pierson and Thomas (2002, p. 376) talk about the process of 'professionalisation' (whereby professions come into being). They explain it as a series of developments:

> A particular skill or area of knowledge emerges in response to changes in economic and social activity; people gather together to exchange ideas and to develop the new territory; if the 'field' has commercial or social potential, the group will increase in number; the members seek to define and set boundaries on the new activity and by so doing seek to distinguish it from associated activities; decisions are made about who can be a member and later a 'practitioner'; and the final stages involve controlling the qualifying process and the conduct of members. The state will incorporate the training of professionals into the mainstream of higher education if the activity is regarded as sufficiently important, although professional organisations will still have some measure of autonomy.

Therefore, in reality, all professions follow their own path, depending upon the context in which they emerge. No profession is exactly the same as the next and neither does it have exactly the same characteristics. Certain aspects of professions also change over time. However, Pierson and Thomas confirm that becoming a recognised profession is the outcome of a 'claims-making' process. The group stakes its claim to socially and/or economically valuable expertise and if this claim is accepted it wins the right to be regarded as the final authority on that particular area of work or knowledge. The last point about state involvement in training is also worth noting. It highlights that while professions might have a relationship with the state in respect of training and, in some cases, fees, the degree to which the state might be said to control any particular profession varies in scope and nature from one profession to the next (Johnson, 1972).

The extent to which social work possesses these characteristics

Above we have reviewed the main criteria that are commonly put forward as defining a profession in the traditional sense. At the same time we have not only noted some of the ambiguities and other points of interest relating to each criterion, but we have also noted that, these days, few, if any, occupational areas could be said to conform completely to the 'classic' template derived from the earliest professions. This leads us onto the point made by Harris and White that social work does not really meet the criteria for a profession as traditionally conceived. They point to the fact that some argue that social work can only be regarded as a 'semi-profession'. Although, they do not define what a semi-profession is at that point.

Several points raised above suggest that social work does not quite fit the description of a classic profession. You might have discussed that this is because it is hard to say exactly what social work's special knowledge base is (that others do not share) or that the profession itself has only limited control over its own affairs in terms of, for example, what it does, who can join the profession and how it is regulated. Compared to professions such as law or medicine, the state plays a very large part in how professional social work is conducted and regulated, suggesting that if it is a profession at all it is a different type of profession. We will discuss all of these issues in more detail in the following chapter when we examine how social work has developed both as an occupation and as a form of profession.

Chapter summary

- The concepts 'profession'; 'professional' and 'professionalism' are constructs and, as such, their meanings are both negotiable and open to different interpretations.
- How we understand concepts such as professional and professionalism depends on the context of when and how they are being used and by whom.
- Professionalism can manifest itself in different ways and take different forms.
- Commonly held interpretations of professional and professionalism associate them with the possession of knowledge, competence and expertise usually acquired through a lengthy training period.
- Beyond competence in the discipline, there is no single list of traits or characteristics that define professionalism. However, most definitions would stress skills in communication as well as demonstrating trustworthy, consistent and ethical practice as essential. The ability to monitor, reflect critically upon and regulate one's own practice is also considered a hallmark of professionalism.
- Discussions about professions or professionalism need to consider matters of power, trust and accountability.

(Continued)

(Continued)

- The concept of professionality – although rarely used – draws our attention to the fact that 'professionalism' can refer to the practices of an individual practitioner but also to the practices of the profession as whole.
- There is no universal agreement on what defines a profession. However, traditional views emphasise independence, the possession of an identifiable body of knowledge and expertise, self-regulation, control over who enters the profession, a code of ethics and a commitment to public/altruistic service.
- Newer professions vary greatly in the extent to which they conform to these criteria. Some refer to social work as a 'semi-profession' for this reason.

Further reading

Abbott, A (1988) *The system of professions: An essay on the division of expert labour*. Chicago: University of Chicago Press.

This book explores the role of professions in modern life generally. It focuses on key questions such as: 'Why should there be occupational groups controlling expert knowledge?' and 'Where and why did groups such as law and medicine achieve their power?'

Crompton, R. (1990) 'Professions in the Current Context', *Work, Employment and Society*, Special Issue: 147–66.

This article examines changing ideas about professions and how they should be regulated.

Epstein, RM and Hundert, EM (2002) Defining and assessing professional competence. *Journal of American Medical Association* (JAMA) 287(2): 226–35.

Often quoted in the literature on professionalism, this article provides a very useful starting place to think about how we can define the characteristics of professional competence.

Etzioni, A. (1969) *The semi-professions and their organization teachers, nurses, social workers*, New York: The Free Press.

This is considered by many to be a seminal text on the 'semi-professions' of teaching, nursing and social work.

Evetts, J (2003) The sociological analysis of professionalism. *International Sociology* 18(2): 395–415.

This article analyses the appeal of the concepts of profession and professionalism and the increased use of these concepts in different occupational groups, work contexts and social systems.

Harris, J and White, V (2013) *A dictionary of social work and social care*. Oxford: Oxford University Press.

This dictionary provides very useful definitions of concepts such as professionalism and profession and how they might or might not relate to social work.

Johnson, T (1972) *Professions and power*. Basingstoke: Macmillan.

This book is considered one of the classic texts on professions and how and where they derive their power.

Parker, J and Doel, M (eds) (2013) *Professional social work*. London: Learning Matters.

This book focuses on key questions about what it is to be professional in the context of social work. Chapter 2 (by Malcom Payne) provides a particularly useful discussion on the professionalisation of social work.

Payne, M (2006) *What is professional social work?* (2nd edn). Bristol: Policy Press.

This authoritative book brings together many key discussions ranging from 'What is a profession?' to why social work has professionalised, as well as examining the impact of professionalising social work.

Pierson, J and Thomas, M (2002) *Collins Dictionary: Social work* (2nd edn). Glasgow: HarperCollins.

As with Harris and White, this dictionary also provides very useful definitions of concepts such as professionalism and profession and how they relate to social work.

2: The Development of Professional Social Work: How We Got to Where We Are

Achieving a social work degree

This chapter will enable you to develop the following capabilities to the appropriate level from the PCF:

- knowledge
- critical reflection and analysis
- contexts and organisations
- professional leadership
- professionalism.

It will also introduce you to the following academic standards as set out in the social work subject benchmark statement:

5.2 Social Work theory
5.3 Values and ethics
5.4 Service users and carers
5.5 The nature of Social Work practice, in the UK and more widely
5.6 The leadership, organisation and delivery of Social Work services
5.17 Skills in personal and professional development

More specifically it will enable you to:

- reflect critically upon the professional status of social work;
- understand developments in the history of professional social work;

- examine critically what have been described as the 'professionalisation', 'deprofessionalisation' and 'reprofessionalisation' of social work;
- appreciate the reasons why 'professional leadership' is now considered to be a key capability of professionalism in the context of contemporary social work.

Introduction

In this chapter, carrying forward ideas about professionalism and what constitutes a profession, we examine the development of professional social work in England. In doing so we will discuss how many of today's social work professional debates, dilemmas and uncertainties have their origins in the very beginnings of social work itself. With notions of professional leadership in mind, it helps to know how we have got to where we are and what the key issues and debates have been along the way when thinking about how to go forward. Examining social work's history helps us to understand both past and contemporary debates about social work's professional status. Focusing on key stages in social work's development, we examine what have been described as the 'professionalisation', 'deprofessionalisation' and 'reprofessionalisation' of social work.

The professional status of social work

While we have seen that social work does not fit the profile of an established profession such as law or medicine it does have certain professional characteristics. Therefore, it could be said to be a profession but with some important qualifications. Earlier we saw social work referred to as a 'semi-profession' by Harris and White (2013). Others have referred to occupations such as teaching and social work as 'state-mediated' professions (Johnson, 1972). Others have argued that social work is a form of 'bureau-profession' (Clarke, 1993; Clarke and Newman, 1997; Harris, 2003). Parker and Doel (2013) have added 'para-profession' to the list. We can better understand the professional status of social work by examining its historical development. This is not a particularly straightforward exercise as any such history will have competing narratives reflecting different interests and perspectives (Doel, 2012). In this respect, two issues can be flagged up immediately. First, it depends what one defines as social work. As Rogowski (2010, p. 27) explains:

> *Actually, what amounts to social work, helping people with problems and difficulties or in need, has always existed; it was carried out by family, friends, neighbours and volunteers. What differentiates social work as a distinct activity is that it can be seen as organised helping originating in organisational responses to social changes arising from socioeconomic developments in the 19th century.*

Second, although many would agree with Rogowski that what starts to become recognisable as modern day social work dates from the mid- to late nineteenth century, as Payne (2005, p. 7) rightly explains, there are 'problems with a single historical narrative'. In fact, there are many organised activities that could be broadly described as social work that date from those times and later. Some have become consolidated into today's social work, others – such as social housing work, probation and education welfare services – have not. Also, many of the activities that were undertaken in previous centuries and do still exist in social work – for example, 'rescuing destitute children from moral danger' – are conceptualised and carried out completely differently these days. The fact that social work's early origins are so diverse and difficult to put boundaries around helps to explain the problems contemporary social work often has in knowing exactly what its main roles and functions are as well as what direction it should be going in. Perhaps the main point to establish at this juncture is that 'social work is shaped by the societal context from which it emerges' (Harris, 2003, p. 3). One of the important tasks of professional leadership is therefore to understand the changing social and economic contexts in which social work takes place and what the drivers for change are.

The emergence of professional social work prior to 1945

Many different social and economic developments took place from the mid- to late nineteenth century through to 1945, when the welfare state was established in the UK, which helped shape the development of social work as a profession. Society itself was changing radically. The population was growing rapidly and becoming more urbanised. The problems of both the urban and rural poor (for example, poverty, squalor, ill-health, alcohol misuse, 'juvenile delinquency' and crime) were becoming more widespread and more complex and needed better informed and more effective solutions in terms of what might be called 'social welfare'. Two important factors from that period that influenced the development of social work were the operation of the Poor Law, 1834, and the work of the Charity Organisation Society (COS) (Payne, 2005; Harris, 2008; Horner, 2012).

In the nineteenth century, much of what could broadly be described as social work was carried out by charitable organisations. However, by the 1860s the number of different charities had proliferated to the point where it was felt that their efforts needed to be properly coordinated, not least because it was feared that some help was going to recipients who were not properly deserving of handouts. The fear was that providing charitable assistance to the 'undeserving', that is to say those who were deemed responsible for their own problems, was only going to encourage dependency, laziness, fecklessness and other forms of immoral behaviour (Ferguson and Woodward, 2009). In 1870 the COS was set up to coordinate efforts and to ensure that only the 'deserving' poor received help. In order to do this the COS recruited 'social case workers' whose role it was to visit applicants and determine whether their lifestyle and circumstances were such that they could be considered eligible (deserving) for charitable assistance (Dustin, 2007; Horner, 2012).

The only state assistance for the poor and needy was, on a local basis via the 1834 Poor Law and was very limited. The role of Poor Law relieving officers was to assess the cases of all those applying for medical or poor relief, to authorise emergency relief or entry into the workhouse. The work of both relieving officers and COS case workers was mainly carried out by well-meaning but judgemental amateurs who took it upon themselves to 'do good' by working 'among' the poor and disadvantaged.

Although people's problems were usually conceptualised as the consequence of individual failings, early social research was demonstrating that poverty and its attendant problems were more due to failings in the economy and in the organisation of society than they were to a lack of morals. In addition to dispensing aid, many charitable organisations were also arguing for social reform. In this respect, Payne (2005) highlights the work of the Settlement movement, among whose goals were educating the poor and campaigning on social policy. The Settlement movement focused more on work at the community rather than individual level (Horner, 2012). Its advocates argued for the state to take more responsibility in the relief of poverty and the social problems it caused (Ferguson and Woodward, 2009). Therefore, in social work's pre-origins we see divisions between those who believed that poverty and its associated problems could be eradicated by reforming the individual and those who argued that the most effective solution was to reform society.

As the nineteenth century gave way to the twentieth century, the extent and complexity of social problems continued to grow. However, there were new ideas about how to understand human behaviour and analyse social problems emerging from the new academic disciplines of social administration, sociology and psychology. In addition, there was also a significant expansion of social legislation and policy (for example, in education, health, crime, social security and child welfare) that needed to be administered and put into practice by a knowledgeable workforce (Page and Silburn, 1999). The modern world was becoming more complex. It was gradually accepted that the old, voluntary, amateur ways of doing things needed to be updated and that, to be effective, more specialist expertise was required. Thus the space and opportunity for new welfare professions opened up.

In the first half of the twentieth century, social work became closely aligned with the expansion of the professions of psychology and psychiatry, and social work training at that time was mainly focused on mental health (Payne, 2005; Healy, 2005; Pierson, 2011). The Association of Psychiatric Social Workers was set up in 1930. It was, however, just one of a diverse range of such 'social work' associations that had grown up around different approaches and different client groups – all of which regarded themselves as separate professions (Pierson, 2011). The emergence of these different associations can be seen as a significant stage in the professionalisation of social work, albeit one that lacked any unity of vision or approach (Payne, 2005).

This very brief summary has demonstrated that 100 years ago professional social work as we know it today did not exist. As Payne (2005) pointed out, there were many different 'social works', some of which have endured and some of which have not and, as Clarke (1993) stated, the many diverse efforts that were being undertaken lacked any real sense of unity of purpose. We conclude this section with an activity that encourages you to think more about professionalism, professionalisation, and how and why social work began to be professionalised.

Activity 2.1

1. Why were there opportunities for social work to become a profession during the period under study?
2. From the definitions provided earlier, why could social work not have been considered to be a profession during this period?

Commentary

There are various reasons why opportunities for the professionalisation of social work opened up in the early twentieth century. They include a growing awareness that the problems facing society were becoming more complex; the acceptance that the mainly amateur thinking and ways of working of the past were no longer effective; the expansion of various types of social legislation that required educated bureaucrats to interpret and put them into practice; and the emergence of new ideas and new forms of knowledge about understanding human behaviour and tackling social problems.

Social work could not be said to be a profession at that time because the activities that might be broadly described as social work were too diverse and fragmented. They encompassed numerous different types of welfare service, many of which were carried out by an unqualified and/or unpaid workforce. There was no agreed, clearly demarcated body of expertise, code of ethics, nor single professional body that could claim to speak for or regulate the workforce.

Social work: 1945–70

After the Second World War, based upon the recommendations of the Beveridge Report, the Labour government introduced a wide programme of social legislation which created the 'welfare state' in the UK (Midwinter, 1994; Lowe, 2005). However, as Harris (2008, p. 7) says, while 'this programme put the major institutions of the welfare state in place; *social work emerged as an afterthought*' [my italics]. As it happened, after the Second World War, state social work developed separately in three broad areas: children's departments, health services and welfare departments. Therefore, the various 'social works' had yet to come together in a unified way. The 'personal social services' as an integrated, demarcated service were not legislated for until 1970, as we shall discuss later. Lowe (2005, p. 273) makes the following observation about social work's development in the post-war decades:

> *Between 1945 and 1975 the personal social services were relatively neglected. They lacked three key qualities:*
>
> * *professional identity*
> * *political weight*
> * *public recognition.*

It would be inaccurate to say that social work lacked an identity altogether. It was beginning to define itself by the underpinning values and principles that informed social casework. These values, such as the need to respect people as individuals and to promote the client's right to self-determination, were drawn from the work of, among others, Perlman (1957); Biestek (1963) and Rogers (1961). However, a profession cannot really define itself by its value base alone (Parker and Doel, 2013).

The uncertainties about professional identity during this period can be illustrated by different views about whether the interests of social workers could be better represented by their trade union or their professional association. During the 1950s and 1960s, as most social workers were local government employees and many were still unqualified, they were as likely to regard their interests as represented by a trade union as they were by membership of a particular professional association – if, indeed, they were eligible to join one. At that point there was no single national organisation that represented all social workers working across all departments (Payne, 2005). This basic difference of opinion underlines the ambiguous status of social workers as 'professionals'. They are qualified professionally and encouraged to see themselves as professionals but, for the most part, they are also salaried employees of public sector bureaucracies.

The Seebohm Report 1968

Social work in the 1960s remained a fragmented and poorly coordinated activity. There was much duplication of efforts between different departments. There was also concern both inside and outside government that there were still significant areas of unmet need in the country, especially among deprived families. In 1965 the government established a Committee chaired by Sir Frederic Seebohm whose terms of reference included 'to review the organisation and responsibilities of local authority personal social services in England and Wales'.

The Seebohm Committee reported in 1968, recommending that the various different elements of personal services should be unified into one organisation under the control of local authorities. The new social services departments were to provide a single, generic, community-based response to the needs of individuals, families and communities. In Seebohm's words they would provide 'one door on which to knock'. The impact of Seebohm on social work was significant. By improving access it increased the demand for social work services. It helped raise social work's standing in the eyes of the public and other professionals. Also, it helped with creating an integrated professional identity among social workers. These were all potentially important steps towards professionalisation. That said, during the 1960s tensions emerged within social work among those who wanted to professionalise around the skills and knowledge of case work (mainly aimed at helping the individual to change) and those who saw professionalisation as a barrier to more community-based, political forms of social work aimed at changing social and economic power structures (Ferguson and Woodward, 2009; Rogowski, 2010).

The recommendations of the Seebohm Report were substantially put into law in the Local Authority Social Services Act 1970. For many this represented the moment when social work 'came of age' as a profession (Langan, 1993). However, the exact status of social work as a fully fledged profession remained uncertain. As Harris (2008, p. 10) says:

> {The Seebohm Report} merged social work's professional identity and the service structure. Social workers were to be neither autonomous professionals nor bureaucratic functionaries; social work was to exist in its own right, within the shell of local government administration, as a form of bureau-professionalism.

As if to underline their ambiguous status as professionals, Ferguson and Woodward (2009, p. 23) observe that trade union membership among social workers rose sharply at that time. They argue that the creation of social services departments helped create a new collective identity among social workers as 'local government *workers*' (their italics).

There is broad agreement that the period following the creation of generic local authority social services departments in 1970 was a landmark for the personal social services in England and for social work. For example, Payne describes this period as 'social work at its zenith' (2005, p. 85) and Langan (1993, p. 48) as the 'high tide of social work'. Rogowski (2010, p. 45) describes the 1960s and 1970s as 'the high watermark of social work'. He lists four developments that, in their own way, contributed to the professionalisation of social work. They are:

- the Children and Young Persons Act 1969 (CYPA)
- the Chronically Sick and Disabled Persons Act 1970 (CSDA)
- the British Association of Social Workers, formed in 1970
- the Central Council for Education and Training in Social Work (CCETSW), formed in 1971.

CYPA 1969 and CSDA 1970

These important Acts invested social workers with a range of new powers and responsibilities, providing them with more opportunities to exercise their professional autonomy. In one sense this underlined the profession's growing professional credibility. However, it brings into focus the key question of how social workers used their growing autonomy. Approaches used by social workers were informed by an eclectic mix of theories and approaches drawn from diverse traditions often supplemented with large amounts of practice wisdom derived from experience and intuition (Sheppard, 1995). The effectiveness of such eclectic approaches was difficult to evaluate, especially as they were often used on an *ad hoc* basis and according to personal preference (Pierson, 2011).

British Association of Social Workers

In 1970, the British Association of Social Workers (BASW) was formed, bringing together medical social workers, psychiatric social workers, childcare officers, moral welfare officers and others. Pierson (2011, p. 122) says that with the creation of generic social services departments (SSDs) BASW gave 'organizational voice to a common vision for social work'. A critical early issue that BASW faced concerned who was actually allowed to join (Payne, 2005; Pierson, 2011). BASW saw itself as a *professional* organisation and many believed that membership should be restricted to qualified staff. However, many social workers at that time were not qualified. Also, holders of the Certificate in Social Service (regarded as a lesser qualification) were not admitted as full members at that point. In the 'radical' 1970s such restrictions on membership were 'seen as a sign of elitism' (Payne, 2005, p. 194). Although now resolved, these disputes underline an enduring ambivalence about what type of profession social work is, and, indeed, whether it should actually be regarded as a profession.

Central Council for Education and Training in Social Work

The CCETSW played an important role in unifying and rationalising professional social work education. It was abolished in 2001, but during its 30 years' existence it played a key role in the professionalisation of social work. It set out the required social work curriculum and controlled entry into the profession. CCETSW was not a body made up purely of professional social workers. It was run by members nominated by the government, employers' organisations, health bodies, educational bodies and professional associations such as BASW. The fact that several stakeholders other than the profession of social work itself played a key role in deciding the social work curriculum is probably another reason why social work is not regarded as a full profession.

To what extent *did* social work become a profession in the 1970s?

It could be argued that by the 1970s social work in England had achieved some, but not all, elements of a recognised profession. In terms of what it had achieved:

- the creation of SSDs following the Seebohm Report raised the profile of social work in recognising that it had an important part to play in the state welfare system. By bringing different workers together from different departments and backgrounds SSDs also helped forge more of a collective identity. Legislation created more powers, roles and responsibilities for social workers, the effects of which also expanded the degree of professional autonomy social workers had in how they discharged their duties;

- diverse professional bodies were consolidated into a single professional association (BASW) which, potentially, gave social work a stronger and more unified voice – for example, in CCETSW. Both BASW and CCETSW had developed ethical codes as both a framework for practice and as an underpinning to social work education;

- training became consolidated around a universally recognised professional qualification: the Certificate of Qualification in Social Work (CQSW). This would be the agreed route into the profession;

- the *British Journal of Social Work* was launched by BASW in 1971. It provides a forum for a broad range of academic and professional knowledge exchange and debate. Its content reflects the diverse, often conflicting, perspectives on social work (Shaw et al., 2016).

In terms of areas where social work's status as a profession remained in doubt:

- while its profile had risen, social work could not be said to enjoy social standing comparable to more established professions such as doctors or lawyers;

- by the 1970s social work was a job substantially created by the state and working for the state. The state provided social work with its 'clientele'. While social workers enjoyed some professional autonomy in how they interpreted the law, in practice, their roles and responsibilities were substantially laid down for them in law, policy guidance and organisational guidelines;

- not all of those working in the various branches of social work were qualified;

- there was no protected status given to the title 'social worker' and there was no professional register from which social workers could be struck off;

- while there was a training period, it was mainly limited to one- and two-year courses. Curriculum content was far from settled and varied from one education provider to another. The knowledge and skills base could not be regarded as either clearly demarcated or evidence-based;

- social work was not self-regulating. Social workers were accountable to their employers (which, as stated above, were mainly state organisations of different types);

- some social workers did actually not want or seek professional status. Those aligned to 'radical social work' feared that the more social work professionalised, the more it risked becoming part of an oppressive state apparatus with social workers acting as 'agents of social control' (Ferguson and Woodward, 2009; Lavalette, 2011).

Summary

Looked at overall, the period from 1945 to the 1970s can be seen as the time when social work became more professional without becoming a fully fledged profession. However, there is no objective evidence to support that social workers' professional competence actually improved during this period. If anything, evidence in many areas suggests a marked lack of professionalism. In the area of child protection for example, there were several tragedies which illustrated, among other things, inadequate communication, poor decision-making and the inability to learn from mistakes (Reder, Duncan and Gray 2005). The residential care system for children and young people has subsequently been found to be the site of widespread institutional abuse (see for example, *Lost in Care*, 2000; Utting, 1991). In other areas of social work, most work with older people was considered low status and low skill and carried out by unqualified and inexperienced staff (Parsloe and Stevenson, 1978). Social work with people with disabilities was often found to be at odds with what service users actually wanted (Shearer, 1981). Mayer and Timms (1970) had already found that there was a significant disparity between social workers and their working-class clients' views about why they were visiting them and what they were supposed to be working on.

Given the growing scale and complexity of the task facing social workers one should not over-look the considerable progress made and paint too bleak a picture of social work. However, if the years from 1945 through to the 1970s are reckoned to be a critical stage in the profes-sionalisation of social work ('social work at its zenith'), then we need to maintain a sense of balance and realism about what was achieved for service users.

1980s and 1990s: The 'deprofessionalisation' of social work?

In 1979 Margaret Thatcher became Prime Minister and set about transforming all aspects of Britain's economy and society. The 1980s and 1990s became critical decades in the transformation of the public sector (Pollitt, 1993; Clarke and Newman, 1997; Page and Silburn, 1999; Harris and White, 2009; Rogowski, 2011). Public sector welfare professionals were viewed with suspicion for making excessive claims of their own expertise in order to 'empire build'. Managers and managerialism was to be the means by which the power of welfare professionals would be curtailed (Lowe, 2005; Parker and Doel, 2013).

By the 1980s social work's standing as a profession had not been helped by the various scandals and failures that continued to come to light and which called standards of professionalism in social work into question. BASW was a relatively weak and divided organisation unable to provide any meaningful professional leadership (Beresford, 2011). Therefore social work was badly placed to resist any attempts by the government to reform it. If that wasn't enough, sections of the media who supported Thatcher were intent on highlighting social work's failings and blaming it for many of the ills of society (Franklin and Parton, 1991). According to Lavalette, (2011, p. 6) social work:

> was increasingly depicted – both by government ministers and the media – as the cause of 'welfare dependency', of 'failed' hippie values, of 'political correctness' and a culture of being 'soft on crime'. In short, social work was portrayed as a 'failed profession'.

The climate for social work to grow into an autonomous, trusted profession of social standing was not propitious.

The management of social work before managerialism

The SSDs created in the 1970s were local government bureaucracies. Management positions throughout were mainly occupied by qualified social workers who had been promoted from the ranks of experienced practitioners. In fact, it was a legal requirement that the director of social services was a qualified social worker (Doel, 2012). Management styles differed from one manager to the next. However, being qualified social workers, their approach tended to be guided by their social work experience, professional values and accumulated practice wisdom. Few, if any, had any specific management qualifications. Generally, they would have had professional allegiances with the workforce. The concept of 'professional leadership' was absent from social work discourse at that time, at least in any official or formal sense. However, being qualified and experienced social workers, most managers acted, either consciously or unconsciously, as professional role models for newly qualified and less experienced practitioners.

Activity 2.2   The impact of managerialism on professional social work

1. Study the two extracts provided below. Note down the features said to characterise social work before and after the introduction of managerialism.
2. Critically reflect upon what you think might be positive and negative effects of these changes for social workers and service users.
3. In what ways could the introduction of managerialism into social work be seen as a process of 'deprofessionalisation'?
4. Think about the implications of managerialisation for professional leadership.

Extract one: White and Harris (2007, pp. 242–3)

'Managerialism' is a term which has been used to describe changes that have taken place in social work and other public (and also, increasingly, voluntary sector) services in recent years in many parts of the world. The core concern of managerialism in the UK, from the early 1980s onwards, was the application of business management structures, systems and techniques to public services, with the objective of getting more for less (Waine and Henderson, 2003, p. 54).

Some of the key features of managerialism are:

- 'management' is a separate and distinct organisational function;
- progress is seen in terms of increasing productivity;
- increased productivity will come from the application of information and organisational technologies;
- there must be a shift from a focus on inputs and processes to outputs and outcomes;
- measurement and quantification need to increase;
- markets or market-type mechanisms should be used to deliver services;
- contractual relationships should be introduced;
- customer orientation should be central;
- the boundaries between the public, private and voluntary sectors should be blurred.

Adapted from Pollitt, 1990, pp. 2–3; 2003, pp. 27–8

Underpinning all of these features of managerialism is the advocacy of greater power for managers; managers have the 'right to manage'. Their role is seen as central to the improvement of organisational performance, which is to be achieved by limiting the discretion of professionals, ostensibly in the interests of empowering the 'customer'.

(Continued)

(Continued)

Extract two: Doel (2012, p. 66)

Managerialism

The introduction of management practices from the private sector into the public sector in the UK began during the Thatcher years (1980s) and has gathered rather than lost momentum. This policy saw managers rather than practitioners becoming the main instrument of social policy. Previously, social work was based on the relationship between the social worker and the client and the success of the work was internally driven – that is, successful work was defined by the worker and client together. However, it became externally driven, with success measured by targets set by the employing agency, which, in turn, reacted to government policies. Even the permissions to start and continue the work became externally driven by 'eligibility criteria' that were determined outside the individual social worker's professional responsibility. This system of micro-management, combined with the practices imported from the profit-driven private sector, is referred to as managerialism.

The managerialist approach prioritises procedures and targets over professional values and standards and it stresses compliance and rule-governed behaviour rather than critical analysis and reflection. Private sector management must capture data about production in order to secure a profit for the shareholders; a similar management strategy in the public sector has tended to value those things that are easy to count, with resources 'objectively' allocated on the basis of these counts. Managerialist practice therefore values quantitative measures over qualitative ones.

Commentary

It is not made clear exactly how social work operated before the introduction of managerialism. However, it is suggested that the work was more relationship-based, less pressurised, with fewer tangibly measured ways of working and with more time for 'critical analysis and reflection'. Others have described this style of social work as more 'organic'. However, after the introduction of managerialism both writers point to how social work became a lot more business-like, proceduralised and focused on performance indicators and 'throughput'. It became a more intensified type of job role, increasingly requiring hitting targets, meeting deadlines, following standardised procedures and spending much more time inputting data into computers. Clients were now to be regarded as 'customers'.

Doel says that, prior to the introduction of managerialism, 'the success of the work was internally driven' and that 'successful work was defined by the worker and client together'. It is implied that social work before managerialism was more focused on 'quality' than 'quantity', with social workers working with more creativity and more autonomy. However, social work, as a profession, was not particularly effective at regulating itself. Quality assurance was very *ad hoc*. Given the power imbalances, the 'success of the work' highlighted by Doel was probably not defined on the service user's terms. Formal feedback mechanisms from service users were practically non-existent. From the service user's perspective, it is quite possible that a degree of standardisation, proceduralisation and greater transparency helped offset the potential for subjectivity and bias that 'organic' styles of working brought with them. So, while it is true to say that social workers had more freedom in how they worked and there was less 'paperwork' with fewer tick-box exercises, there is no conclusive evidence to suggest that standards of professionalism were higher or that the social work prior to managerialisation led to greater service user satisfaction or better outcomes.

In thinking about whether the introduction of managerialism into social work could be seen as a process of 'deprofessionalisation', we need to remember that social work had not actually fully professionalised. However, if we focus on the degree of professional autonomy available to social workers, this was certainly constrained. That said, the nature of the work means it cannot be completely deskilled and routinised (Lipsky, 1980). While the work of practitioners and managers became subject to closer surveillance and tighter controls, the space for professional discretion remained. Managerialism curtailed professional autonomy significantly, but did not eradicate it completely (Evans and Harris, 2004; Evans, 2010). Managerialisation played out in different ways in different organisations and services (Clarke and Newman, 1997). Some branches of social work were more susceptible to managerialisation than others. Adult services, in particular, became very managerialised following the implementation of the NHS and Community Care Act 1990 (Lymbery and Postle, 2007; Rogowski, 2010; Bamford, 2015). In fact, the role of social worker became replaced by that of 'care manager'. Care management was a highly proceduralised role mainly based around assessing eligibility for care 'packages' (Postle, 2002). While this transformation can be largely attributed to the way 'community care' was conceived of and implemented by the government, the deprofessionalisation of adult social work can also be explained by the fact that much of the work with older and disabled people was not particularly professionalised to begin with.

As far as the implications for professional leadership went, social work managers in the 1980s and 1990s became more focused on budgets and meeting organisational targets rather than discussing professional social work issues or taking a professional leadership role. This was not necessarily by choice; it was the result of policy directives. The bigger picture was for all public services to become privatised in some shape or form and to be run according to business principles. Managers needed to enforce this agenda and this is how their effectiveness was judged. Management training was all about achieving the three 'E's' – Economy, Efficiency and

Effectiveness (Harris and White, 2009). While managerialism notionally improved productivity it did not necessarily improve quality. By shifting control to managers (many of whom were now not qualified social workers), together with the responsibility for meeting targets, SSDs were much less likely to be the sites for discussion on professional social work issues. As a consequence of managerialisation, social work managers' allegiances were more likely to be to their employing organisation than to social work professional values. This meant that their capacity for professional leadership became compromised if it did not disappear altogether. In general, social services managers were no longer role modelling professional social work.

Social work's 'critical' turn

Managerialism had a major impact on professional social work in the 1980s and 1990s; however, there are other important developments to note that took place in those decades. Social work embraced 'criticality'. Criticality can have different meanings (Adams, Dominelli and Payne, 2009). However, broadly speaking, when applied to social work, the concept is well encapsulated by Parker and Doel (2013, p. 211), who describe it as 'a kind of self-researching exercise ... in which social workers interrogate their own working hypotheses'. There are two broad dimensions of 'criticality' to note.

The critically reflective practitioner

Drawing on learning theories and taking the lead from other professions such as teaching, social work embraced the idea of the (critically) reflective practitioner. Informed by the writings of, among others, Argyris (1976); Schön (1983) and Brookfield (1987), this approach to practice was about developing exactly the professional 'habits of mind' identified by Epstein and Hundert (2002). Key skills included being able to look at oneself critically and identify and manage subjective factors such as any prejudices, biases, fears or anxieties that might impair clarity of thought and decision-making. These skills also required being able to put oneself and one's worldview into context. Critical thinking and reflective practice are now considered the cornerstones of professional social work for various reasons (Rutter and Brown, 2011; Knott and Scragg, 2016). They are also vital for professional leadership, as we shall discuss later.

Critical practice

Critical practice also requires the ability to 'situate' oneself socially. It is a broad description that covers social work's ability to utilise sociological theories to understand, for example, how power structures, oppression, discrimination and marginalisation in society works. To a degree, it evolved out of the radical social work of the 1970s (Payne, 2006). The important point for critical practice is not only to avoid reproducing power imbalances, but also to challenge the structures that maintain them. Critical practice came about from a growing awareness of the different bases of oppression in society: race; class; gender; disability; sexuality; age; and so on. The academic impetus for this change came from critical theory (Adams et al., 2009; Fook, 2002). However, the incorporation of forms of critical practice into social work was, in no small measure, in response to campaigning from 'new social movements' at a time when new forms of 'identity politics' were emerging (Payne, 2005; Cowden and Singh, 2007; Smith, 2008; Beresford, 2011; Lavalette, 2011). In a similar way, the adoption of the social model of disability followed pressure from the disability movement (Oliver and Sapey, 2006). This switched the focus of social work away from concentrating on the individual's deficits to addressing the disabling features of the social and physical environment. The growing receptivity to 'bottom up' movements saw social work gradually accepting the view that 'service users' – in all their diversity – should have a stronger individual and collective voice in decisions affecting them (BASW, 1980; Cowden and Singh, 2007). It's a vague term, often used glibly, but the 1980s could be regarded as the decade when social work embraced the concept of 'empowerment' (Singh and Cowden, 2013).

Social work academics were probably ahead of the social work workforce in the zeal with which they embraced critical practice. However, once it had become established in social work education during the 1980s and 1990s, anti-discriminatory, anti-racist and anti-oppressive practice became embedded in social work practice generally (Laird, 2008; CCETSW, 1989). Critical practice could be said to epitomise social work's basic ambivalence about which way to go forward as a 'profession'. While undoubtedly committed to improved standards of service, critical practice is a rejection of traditional professional approaches, requiring, as it does, a more democratic, power-sharing and empowering relationship between social worker and service user.

Social work in the twenty-first century: Reprofessionalisation?

The final stage that we will we examine in this historical overview is the period from 2000 onwards. By 2000 the 'New' Labour government had been in power for three years. When they were first elected New Labour talked about taking a 'Third Way'. This was proposed as a distinct middle path between the Conservative 'New Right' and 'old' Labour approaches that had gone before. The guiding principle was supposedly 'what matters is what works'. However, New Labour continued the privatisation, marketisation and managerialisation of public services under the programme heading of 'modernisation' (Department of Health, 1998; Cabinet Office, 1999). Modernisation also required government and public services to be more 'joined-up' (Newman, 2001). Alongside this large programme of reform, several other events influenced social work. Key landmarks are summarised in broad chronological order below.

Timeline of key landmarks

1998 Modernising social services

The White Paper *Modernising social services* (Department of Health, 1998) contained a long list of areas where social services were considered to be failing (including the failure to protect the most vulnerable in society). Many reforms were pledged, including better training and new systems of regulation involving extensive indicators and standards against which 'quality', 'value', 'performance' and 'efficiency' would be measured. As well as more extensive systems of regulation, modernisation required improved 'partnership working' between services, but also with 'the public', who were encouraged to be more active in helping themselves (Newman and Clarke, 2009). The impact on social work was more emphasis on partnership working, but also a greater focus on meeting performance indicators (Kirkpatrick, 2006). Underpinning all of this was an ever greater use of ICT systems. The result was a significant intensification in the way the job was carried out (Jordan, 2001; Harris and White, 2009; Rogowski, 2011).

2000/2003 Victoria Climbié/Laming

The twenty-first century began with yet another death of a child known to social services – that of eight-year-old Victoria Climbié. All the main agencies involved in the multi-agency child protection system attracted criticism in the subsequent inquiry and report (Laming, 2003). The Laming Report made 108 recommendations, 45 of which were aimed specifically at 'social care'. Frontline professionals were criticised – among other things, for a failure to follow basic practice guidelines, to share and communicate important information with each other and, at times, for a lack of courage. The bulk of Laming's social care recommendations were directed towards directors of social services and other senior managers, reflecting the many criticisms of managers contained in the report. Managers were not only blamed for failing to take proper responsibility for the dysfunctional and poorly resourced way in which their organisations were running, but they were also castigated for failure to provide leadership. Most, but not all, of Laming's recommendations were implemented in some form or another. However, even prior to the report being published, the New Labour government had already set in train several policies that would impact on social work generally and on children services in particular. The first piece of legislation that had a significant impact was the Care Standards Act 2000.

2000 The Care Standards Act

The Care Standards Act 2000 contained a range of provisions concerning the regulation of social care. The Act introduced a new, independent regulatory body for social care: the National Care Standards Commission and established the General Social Care Council for England.

2001 The General Social Care Council

The General Social Care Council (GSCC) became the social care workforce regulator for England. The role of the council was to register social care workers, regulate the training of social workers and raise standards in social care through new codes of conduct and practice. It took over CCETSW's responsibilities as regulator of social work education.

2001 Social Care Institute for Excellence

The remit of Social Care Institute for Excellence (SCIE) was to review research and practice in social care, establishing a database of good, evidence-based methods and services. However, note the replacement of the term social *work* by social *care* in many official bodies at this time (Rogowski, 2011). This contributed to a sense that social work in itself did not occupy a special or distinct role in the welfare system.

2002 Department of Health requires service users to be involved in social work education

The Department of Health (2002) required social work education providers to ensure that representatives of stakeholders (particularly service users and employers) were involved in their course selection and assessment processes.

2002 General Social Care Council publishes Code of practice for social care workers

These codes were a key step in the introduction of a system of regulation for social care in England. It was a key requirement for registration that all practitioners signed up to the *Code of practice for social care workers*. This also applied to social work students.

2003 The General Social Care Council begins to register social care workers

The intention was for all social care workers to register with the GSCC. The process began with qualified social workers who could sign up on a voluntary basis. After a slow take-up, the government later declared that only those on the GSCC register could use the designation of social worker.

2003 Social work degree

The three-year degree replaced the two-year Diploma in Social Work as the qualifying route into social work in England. The requirements for the new degree stipulated that certain core subject areas had to be covered (Department of Health, 2002). These included:

- human growth and development, mental health and disability;
- assessment planning, intervention and review;
- communication skills with children, adults and those with particular communication needs;
- law; and
- partnership working and information sharing across agencies and disciplines.

No mention was made about the need to cover any form of leadership, professional or otherwise.

2004 Children Act

The Children Act 2004 was introduced largely as a result of the Laming Report into the death of Victoria Climbié. It brought all local government functions of children's welfare and education under the statutory authority of local directors of children's services. This effectively ended generic SSDs and reinforced the organisational split between adults' and children's social work which had begun in the 1990s.

2004 Social Work Action Network formed

Proclaiming that 'social work in Britain today has lost direction', a loose group of workers, academics and service users, formed the Social Work Action Network (SWAN) (Ferguson and Woodward, 2009). Among other aims, SWAN set out: 'To challenge the domination of social work and social care services by managerialist perspectives and practices which prioritise budgets, targets and outcomes over the needs of the people who use these services' (http://www.socialworkfuture.org/who-we-are/constitution).

2005 Post-qualifying framework for social work education and training revised

The GSCC (2005) launched a new Post-qualifying (PQ) framework comprising three levels of awards: Specialist; Higher Specialist; and Advanced. Specialisms were planned in: mental health; adult social services; practice education; leadership and management; and children and young people, their families and carers.

2008 Death of 'Baby P' (Peter Connelly)

Seventeen-month-old Peter Connelly died in the London Borough of Haringey due to severe abuse and neglect by his mother and her male acquaintances. An emergency inspection of child protection services in Haringey revealed many failings in the children's safeguarding system, including inconsistent quality of frontline practice and poor information recording and sharing. Ed Balls, the Children's Secretary, set up the Expert Group on the Children's Workforce to look at the problems facing social work. The Expert Group proposed that a Social Work Task Force be set up to examine frontline social work practice and 'advise how improvements should be made to social worker training, recruitment and leadership' (Department for Children, Schools and Families, 2008, p. 7).

2008 Reclaiming Social Work launched in London Borough of Hackney

The Reclaiming Social Work (RSW) model (also known as the Hackney model) was aimed at children and families social work. It was co-founded by Goodman and Trowler through the social enterprise Morning Lane Associates (Goodman and Trowler, 2012). It has subsequently been adopted in various forms by other local authorities. According to the Morning Lane website (http://morninglane.org/): 'The model is predicated on the core belief that social work – as a profession – has lost its way: it lacks confidence, expertise and gravitas, and is over-bureaucratised.'

RSW is based around a multi-disciplinary team headed by a consultant social worker working to a systems approach. The official evaluation praised the model for the clarity of its theoretical base, the emphasis on supervision, small teams, limited workloads, reflection and a relationship-based approach (Forrester et al., 2013). That said, Jones (2015) has highlighted how the model can go awry if all parts of the system are not in place – which, unfortunately, is quite often.

2009 The Social Work Task Force is set up

The Social Work Task Force (SWTF) was made up of social work leaders, academics, charity representatives and a journalist from the *Sun* newspaper. Its first interim report highlighted: weak leadership, the lack of a national voice, poor IT support and excessive bureaucracy. The second interim report called for the formation of a national college for social work. It also recommended a national career structure, action on supervision and workloads, and stronger partnerships between employers and universities. The final report of the SWTF (2009) made 15 recommendations for a comprehensive reform programme. The Social Work Reform Board was set up to drive the reforms. Noting that 'social workers are unsure about where to look for leadership of their profession' (ibid., p. 45), the SWTF made the following recommendation:

> *We are recommending the establishment of an independent national college of social work. The college will articulate and promote the interests of good social work. It will give the profession itself strong, independent leadership; a clear voice in public debate, policy development and policy delivery; and strong ownership of the standards to be upheld.*
>
> Ibid., p. 8

2009 Laming's national review of child protection

Lord Laming's review of child protection in England called for an overhaul of social work training and management. It found that children's social workers were suffering from 'low staff morale, poor supervision, high case-loads, and under-resourcing' (Laming, 2009, p. 44). While the Children's Secretary accepted all 58 of Laming's recommendations, not all of them found their way into policy. Nevertheless, it was generally felt that the reforms would lead to significant changes to the practice, training, management and status of social workers.

2009 General Social Care Council criticised

The Chief Executive of the General Social Care Council was suspended after it emerged that a backlog of 203 professional misconduct cases had not been properly dealt with. A review by the Council for Healthcare Regulatory Excellence was highly critical of how the regulation of social workers' professional conduct was being managed.

2010 Conservative and Liberal Democrat Coalition government elected: austerity

Following the financial crisis of 2007–8 a period of economic recession began in the UK. The first austerity measures (cutbacks in public spending and raising taxes) were introduced in late 2008. However, the Conservative and Liberal Democrat Coalition government made austerity one of their top priorities when formed in May 2010. It is argued that this raised the demand for social work while cutting back on the resources needed to respond (Jordan and Drakeford, 2012).

2010 Social Work Reform Board

The Social Work Reform Board (SWRB) was established to carry out the recommendations of the SWTF. The Board was keen to hear what employers wanted but drew on a variety of submissions, including the recommendations of the *Munro review of child protection* (see below) to come to its conclusions. The SWRB produced three reports. Its chief recommendations came in *Building a safe and confident future: One year on* (Social Work Reform Board, 2010). This report underlined the SWRB's commitment to ensuring the continuing professional development (CPD) of social workers through an overarching PCF consisting of nine capability 'domains'. The ninth domain was 'Professional Leadership', which required social workers at all stages of their careers to develop and demonstrate leadership (McGregor, 2011). Having reported, the SWRB was finally disbanded in September 2013.

2010 Launch of Step Up to Social Work: First graduate fast track scheme

Step Up to Social Work was an initiative to recruit graduates into children and family social work from other careers. It was designed to deal with problems with recruitment and retention and also improve the calibre of the workforce. The curriculum followed is based around the PCF, but is devised by regional partnerships of councils and higher education institutions (HEIs).

More controversially, in 2013, another graduate fast track scheme – Frontline – was launched. It too was aimed at raising the standard of children and family social work. Much of the controversy is centred upon the fact that the curriculum followed is not as broad as that followed in conventional routes, raising concerns as to whether it actually meets the Health and Care Professions Council (HCPC) requirements. However, as part of its course Frontline does have a 'leadership development programme' whose aims are 'to help develop the leadership qualities needed to bring about change with families, within the social work profession and beyond' (Frontline, http://www.thefrontline.org.uk/our-programme/frontline-programme-details/leadership-development).

2011 The Munro review of child protection

In 2010 the Coalition government commissioned a review of safeguarding practice by Professor Eileen Munro of the London School of Economics (LSE). Munro consciously took a 'systems approach' to understanding what went wrong and produced three reports altogether. In her first report, Munro (2010a) highlighted several issues including: high caseloads, limited supervision, not enough emphasis on reflective practice, analytical thinking and professional decision-making; and also IT systems that were not fit for purpose. The interim report (Munro, 2010b, p. 34) among other things, highlighted that social work needed: 'stronger leadership and independence – with the profession taking more control over its own standards'.

In her final report Munro argued that social work had become too bureaucratised. She recommended that centrally imposed targets and regulations be scrapped, and that children's social workers be given the freedom to exercise their professional skills and judgement (Munro, 2011). The following extracts indicate what Munro says about the 'role of leadership' (ibid., pp. 106, 106–7):

> *7.6 Leadership will be needed throughout organisations to implement the review's recommendations successfully, especially to help move from a command-and-control culture encouraging compliance to a learning and adapting culture.*

> *7.7 Leadership behaviours should be valued and encouraged at all levels of organisations. At the front line, personal qualities of leadership are needed to work with children and families when practising in a more professional, less rule-bound, way.*

Also in regard to leadership, Munro called for the government to establish a Chief Social Worker in England 'to advise ministers on what they can do to assist social workers in improving practice' (ibid., p. 105). Munro goes on to say: 'At present, in England, there is no permanent professional presence for social work within Government, despite the fact that Government policy can fundamentally influence social work practice, and the service that people receive' (ibid., p. 118).

Finally, linked to the Chief Social Workers' role, Munro proposed the creation of principal social workers (PSWs), who were to become champions of social work practice within local authorities. Principal social worker networks were facilitated by The College of Social Work.

Overall, the PSW has a key professional leadership role. Their role includes: improving standards; maintaining direct links with practice; developing circles of influence; networking outside their local authority; being visible and being a conduit through which practice can speak to management and vice versa. Subsequent reaction to how these roles have functioned in practice shows a mixed picture, with some feeling that the role was in danger of becoming another tool of managerialism rather than a champion for the profession (*Community Care*, 2015b; 2017b).

2012 The College of Social Work

The College of Social Work (TCSW) emerged from the recommendations of the SWTF (2009) and was endorsed by the *Munro review*. The aim was to raise standards and offer a strong, independent, social worker-led voice for the profession. The expectation was that most of its income would come from fee-paying members. But throughout the College's existence, the number of fee-paying members did not reach the number required to put it on a sound financial footing. Apart from financial problems, TCSW had a troubled and uneasy relationship with BASW over a range of issues (Bamford, 2015). This 'row', according to Bamford (ibid., p. 160), was 'damaging to social work' and showed social work to be 'a divided profession'.

The creation of TCSW gave social workers (and students) three main organisations to represent their interests: TCSW, BASW (including the Social Workers Union [SWU]) and UNISON. In 2012, TCSW had just started recruiting, BASW had just over 14,000 and UNISON over 40,000 members. Each claimed to speak for social work and promote the interests of social workers (*Community Care*, 2012). On one level, it could be argued that the fact that there were three organisations reflected the 'broad church' of social work and provided choice. However, on another level, it could be regarded as further evidence that social work lacks a single, unified, independent and authoritative voice to speak for it.

TCSW closed in 2015 (see below).

2012 Closure of the General Social Care Council

The GSCC was abolished by the Coalition government in July 2012. The regulation of social workers was taken over by the newly expanded HCPC. Somewhat confusingly, in addition to the PCF, the HCPC introduced its own 15 'standards of proficiency' for social workers (HCPC, 2012), which then had to be mapped against the PCF.

2013 A Chief Social Worker for Children and Families and a Chief Social Worker for Adults

In September 2013 Isabelle Trowler and Lyn Romeo started their new roles as Chief Social Worker for Children and Families and Chief Social Worker for Adults respectively. According to GOV.UK (2013) their role was to:

- support and challenge the profession to ensure that children and adults get the best possible help from social workers;
- provide independent expert advice to ministers on social work reform and the contribution of social work and social workers to policy implementation more generally;
- provide leadership and work with key leaders in the profession and wider sector to drive forward the improvement and reform programme for social work;
- challenge weak practice to achieve decisive improvements in the quality of social work;
- provide leadership to the network of PSWs to improve practice and influence national policy making and delivery.

It was hoped by many that these roles would enable the voice of professional social work to be heard at government level. Subsequently, in response to criticism at a BASW conference, Isabelle Trowler admitted 'I don't pretend I am the voice of the profession. I am a civil servant' (Children and Young People Now, 2016). This confirmed fears that a significant part of the chief social worker (CSW) role appeared to be putting the government's view to the profession rather than the other way round.

2015 Demise of The College of Social Work

TCSW was closed by the Conservative government, ostensibly for financial reasons (see case study 2.1). However, Beresford (2015) regarded its closure 'as symbolic of a much deeper ideological struggle with the government and a weakening and restructuring of the profession'. Ironically, given their long-running disputes about, among other things, who represented the voice of the profession, BASW was asked to take over management of the PCF.

Case study 2.1   The closure of TCSW

The College of Social Work is to close due to a lack of funds after less than four years in operation. . . . The government said the decision to stop funding The College had not been taken lightly. On social media Isabelle Trowler, the Chief Social Worker for Children, said that The College's financial situation was such that it was "not tenable" for the government to keep "ploughing in" funds.

Jo Cleary, chair of The College, told Community Care: "I'm devastated with the government's decision about the future of The College of Social Work. This is a very dark day for social work and for the people that social workers support. There has never been a more critical time for social work to be a well-regarded and well-respected profession. The College is very proud of what it has achieved over its very short life." She added: "We will make sure that the resources we have produced and the functions that we do have will have a safe and successful transition."

The College was established as an independent body in 2012 with £5m in government seed funding. . . . The organisation's aim was to raise standards and offer a strong, independent, social worker-led voice for a troubled profession in desperate need of reform. The hope was that almost all of its income would come from fee-paying members. But throughout the College's existence, the number of fee-paying members remained well short of what was required to put it on a firm financial footing. The College's target was to have 31,000 fee-paying members by 2015. In April, it had 16,471 but that included social workers who had been signed up by their local authorities via a 'corporate membership scheme' introduced in a bid to boost income.

The shortage of membership income led to an over-reliance on funding from central government contracts and local authority cash through corporate memberships. There have also been signs that politicians' belief in The College has been waning, certainly among policy makers in charge of children's social care.

Community Care, 2015a (abridged)

2014 Croisdale-Appleby and Narey reviews into social work education

In 2013 two different government ministers from different government departments commissioned separate reviews of social work education. Following the work of the SWRB and SWTF, the Minister of State for Health invited Professor David Croisdale-Appleby (who was chair of Skills for Care) to conduct an independent review of social work education. More or less at the same time, the Secretary of State for Education asked Sir Martin Narey (a former

Director of Prisons and government advisor on adoption) to review the initial education of children's social workers. The two did not consult each other.

Croisdale-Appleby

Croisdale-Appleby (2014) made 22 recommendations, including: higher entry requirements for social work courses, a reduction in the number of social workers trained and the development of a new strategic workforce planning system, and social workers facing a 'fitness to practise' test at least every five years once qualified. Croisdale-Appleby says very little specifically about professional leadership per se. However, he did state that those in leadership positions in the profession should act more effectively to challenge the 'facile scapegoating' that social work traditionally faces in the media and elsewhere (ibid., p. 81).

Narey

Compared to Croisdale-Appleby, who was praised for his methodological rigour, Narey (2014) was more selective in the sources upon which he based his review. Nevertheless, he was scathing about many aspects of social work education. Generally, he found that the calibre of those entering social work education was often not good enough; that the system of education offered in universities did not sufficiently prepare students to function effectively in practice; and that some of those graduating lacked the most basic of skills – for example, written communication. He made 18 recommendations. They included the observation that the HCPC authorisation of social work degrees and TCSW's endorsement scheme for social work degrees were both inadequate and needed to be replaced by a single and robust system of inspection; that TCSW should become the single inspector of social work training courses and take on a full regulatory role.

Overall, while generating much debate and making several valid points, neither of the reports was completely embraced nor its recommendations fully implemented. As three senior social work academics lamented 'the result has been muddle and confusion' (Thoburn, Featherstone and Morris 2017).

2014 The launch of Knowledge and skills statements

In November 2014 the Department of Education (DfE) published the *Knowledge and skills statement for approved child and family practitioners*. Largely developed by Isabelle Trowler, the Chief Social Worker, it was said to be designed to build public respect and confidence for social workers 'by ensuring that every child and family social worker is properly supported to do the job society needs them to do'.

This was followed in November of the next year by the *Knowledge and skills statements for practice leaders and practice supervisors* (Department of Education, 2015). The latter document was devised by a consortium led by the professional service company KPMG and included the University of Leeds and Morning Lane Associates. This process attracted some criticism at the time (see, for example, SWAN, 2017). However, as the government website (GOV.UK, 2015) explained:

These statements will form the basis of the new national accreditation system for child and family social workers. They are for:

- *frontline practitioners (staff)*
- *practice supervisors*
- *practice leaders*

Practice supervisors are qualified social workers responsible for:

- *supervising approved child and family social workers*
- *developing the skills of teams and individuals involved in child and family social work services*

Practice leaders are qualified social workers responsible for:

- *making sure the whole local system for child and family social work practice operates correctly*
- *overseeing approved child and family social workers and practice supervisors.*

In March, the Department of Health (2015) published the *Knowledge and skills statement* [KSS] *for social workers in adult services.*

Overall, the various KSSs were expected to both complement the PCF and help to drive up standards of practice in the areas specified. As we have seen, they have brought practice leadership more to the fore, albeit in the context of a senior management role. More will be discussed about the implications for professional leadership of these statements in later chapters.

Conclusion

This chapter has covered a lot of ground and not always in the greatest of depth. Therefore, a suggested selected reading list is provided at the end. However, its aim has been to flesh out the broad social, economic and political contexts in which social work takes place, as well as highlighting key developments in legislation and policy. In this overview we have seen how social work has a complex history comprising many different strands. We have seen how, throughout its history, social work has struggled to achieve the status of a recognised profession. It has also struggled to agree on what its roles and responsibilities should be and settle upon an agreed direction along which it should travel. There have been many documented examples where social work has failed those it is supposed to serve, suggesting that it requires a better-trained, -skilled and -regulated workforce. However, in addition, we have seen how what the social work curriculum should cover and how it should be taught has divided opinion (and still does). We have also seen how, because of the complex nature of the task, social work has come to recognise the need to work in partnership and to draw on a range of knowledge from different sources (Pawson et al., 2003). Accordingly, as well as the move towards 'evidence-based' practice, the input of service users and carers is now actively sought.

We have seen how managerialism has notionally tried to raise productivity and standards, but has hardly been successful in achieving either of these goals, especially against a backdrop of severely constrained public spending. Social work managers, generally, have not always proved effective in leading on social work principles and values, although, in recent years, new leadership roles have been created. It has been pointed out that the regulatory framework in which social work takes place has changed frequently, partly in response to perceived failings but also due to political decision-making. Unlike the more established professions, social work has not been trusted to regulate itself. In fact, nearly all of the reports commissioned and initiatives instigated to improve social work have been externally driven rather than coming from within social work itself (McKitterick, 2015).

Having become 'generic' in the 1970s, the personal social services have now fragmented into various specialisms. Several reports and studies have highlighted the ongoing problems social work has with speaking with a confident and collective professional voice; providing a coherent vision of what social work is and where it should be going; maintaining professional standards and creating a professional identity that helps both those working in it and those on the outside respect social work for the contribution it makes. Commentators have lamented that social work seems to have lost its direction. The exact direction in which social work will go is uncertain. However, at this stage in its history, we can be sure that certain inescapable points need to be heeded.

First, social work is significantly constrained by legislative, bureaucratic and organisational factors, as well as limited resources. Not only is it almost exclusively state funded, but the state also determines who its service users will be. For these reasons, although social workers have powers, they have very limited professional autonomy.

Second, perhaps more than any other profession, social work is acutely aware of the power that it wields and has committed itself to be more democratic whenever it can. As a consequence, social work is open to knowledge-sharing, working in partnership and in collaboration with its various stakeholders, particularly service users and carers. On the one hand, this can be considered to be one of social work's main strengths, but, on the other, in a profession that lacks both confidence and a strong identity, this can result in social work forever being defined by and fitting in around the views and opinions of others. This presents one of the bigger challenges of professional leadership. Social work needs to be better at knowing and communicating what its core functions are, what it is good at and what its particular usefulness is in the welfare system. If it cannot do that, why should anyone else respect the profession? An appropriate balance therefore needs to be struck between being attentive to and respectful of the opinions of others and being assertive about the important functions social work carries out on behalf of society and, as a consequence of this, the valuable expertise that social work brings to the table as a welfare profession.

Third, social work also needs to be better at regulating and policing itself – that is to say, maintaining proper standards of professionalism – or else it will always be vulnerable to criticisms from outside and forever find itself having to fall in with the recommendations and agendas of others.

Lastly, social work might well benefit from being more realistic and pragmatic about what it can actually achieve as an occupation of predominantly public sector workers working with scarce resources trying, much of the time, to manage hugely complex situations. 'Promoting social change and development, social cohesion, and the empowerment and liberation of people' (IFSW, 2014) are laudable aspirations and ones with which social work should certainly associate itself. However, whether these goals should define the 'profession' arguably make it a hostage to fortune.

That is not an exhaustive list of questions facing social work by any means. However, the issues raised above require leadership from within social work itself in order to resolve them in ways that are actually achievable and that social workers themselves can buy into. In so doing, one would hope that this would allow the profession to feel at ease with itself, maintain and restore public confidence, move forward with a sense of purpose and continue to make a vital contribution in society.

We have seen that leadership has often been found to be lacking at various times and in various contexts. There is no single body that includes all social workers and speaks on their behalf. The concept of professional leadership has arrived on the agenda comparatively recently and for various reasons. While it is still assumed that much professional leadership will remain with senior figures such as the CSWs, PSWs and practice leaders, the *Munro report* and the PCF make it clear that those at every level need to take some responsibility in this area. This inevitably raises the questions of how and to what ends? The answers to these and other relevant questions will form the basis for the remaining chapters.

Chapter summary

....

- The roots of today's social work are many and various and can be traced back to at least the nineteenth century. Early social work evolved from, among other things, the influence of the Poor Law, the COS and the Settlement movement.
- From the start, there have been differences of opinion about what form social work should take, with some doubting the wisdom of professionalisation.

- The changes in social work that occurred in the 1980s and 1990s present a mixed picture in terms of its development as a profession. Social work became more 'critical', embracing both reflective and critical practice. Anti-racist, anti-discriminatory and anti-oppressive practice also became embedded in social work education and worked their way into practice.

- Managerialisation used IT systems to bring more standardisation, proceduralisation and target setting into social work. As a consequence, social work became a more closely monitored and intensified job. Although managerialisation gave more power to managers and controlled the extent to which practitioners could work autonomously, it did not eradicate practitioner discretion altogether.

- Managerialism shifted social managers' allegiances to their employing organisation and away from professional values. That, coupled with an ineffective professional association, meant that professional leadership during this period suffered from a lack of direction.

- Social work has accepted the need to become more responsive to service users. Grass roots campaigners demanded the right for power to be shared, while government agendas required public services to be more 'customer focused'.

- Social work in England in the twenty-first century takes place in the context of a public sector that has been subject to decades of privatisation, marketisation, managerialisation and cutbacks.

- New Labour's programme of 'modernisation' led to more extensive regulatory regimes, including a register for qualified social workers; greater use of ICT, targets and more 'joined-up' thinking and working.

- The tragic deaths of children known to social services have led to reforms designed to improve standards of professionalism in key areas: use of evidence, collaborative working, the assessment and management of risk, use of professional judgement in decision-making.

- Legislative, policy and organisational changes have meant that children's and adults' social work have become separated. The publication of KSSs and the emergence of fast track qualifications for children's social work reflect how social work is becoming a profession of specialisms rather than being a generic occupation.

- Several reviews and reports have highlighted that social work has problems with excessive bureaucracy and unresponsive management. They have also noted that social work lacks leadership at all levels. In connection with this perceived lack of professional leadership, TCSW was created, together with CSWs and PSWs.

- Reports on social work education have produced divergent views about what direction the profession should be going in.

- The PCF stresses the need for practitioners at all levels, including students, to demonstrate professional leadership.

Further reading

Bamford, T (2015) *Contemporary history of social work: Learning from the past*. Bristol: Policy Press.

This well-informed book provides an understanding of social work's development as a profession while helping the reader to better understand contemporary debates within social work.

Harris, J (2008) State social work: Constructing the present from moments in the past. *British Journal of Social Work* 38(4): 662–79.

This article focuses on five historical 'moments' that have had significant implications for social work's development in the UK. They are: the nineteenth-century origins of social work; social work in the post-war period; the Seebohm Report; the New Right; and New Labour.

Horner, N (2012) *What is social work?* (4th edn). London: Sage/Learning Matters.

This book provides a very accessible account of how the main branches of social work evolved in the UK.

Parker, J and Doel, M (eds) (2013) *Professional social work*. London: Learning Matters.

This book explores key questions about what it means to be professional in the context of social work. Chapter 2 (by Malcom Payne) provides a particularly useful discussion on the professionalisation of social work.

Payne, M (2005) *The origins of social work*. Basingstoke: Macmillan Palgrave.

This book provides a well-researched account of the history of social work. It sets out the diverse factors, issues and challenges that have shaped the profession of social work as we know it today. It includes a welcome international perspective to understanding the development of social work.

Pierson, J (2011) *Understanding social work: History and context*. Maidenhead: Open University Press.

As with Payne, Pierson's is a scholarly but accessible book that explains the diverse origins of contemporary social work. Both books provide a comprehensive set of references for those who want to pursue this fascinating subject in more depth.

Rogowski, S (2010) *Social work: The rise and fall of a profession?* Bristol: Policy Press.

Rogowski provides a critical analysis of social work's historical development as a profession. Coming from a radical perspective, Rogowski is particularly critical of the (negative) impact of managerialism and neoliberalism on social work.

3: Leadership and Followership: Definitions, Theories and Models

Achieving a social work degree

This chapter will enable you to develop the following capabilities to the appropriate level from the PCF:

- knowledge
- critical reflection and analysis
- intervention and skills
- contexts and organisations
- professional leadership
- professionalism.

It will also introduce you to the following academic standards as set out in the social work subject benchmark statement:

5.2   Social Work theory
5.3   Values and ethics
5.4   Service users and carers
5.5   The nature of Social Work practice, in the UK and more widely
5.6   The leadership, organisation and delivery of Social Work services
5.17 Skills in personal and professional development

More specifically it will enable you to:

- explore different definitions and ideas about leaders and leadership
- review potential leadership roles

(Continued)

(Continued)

- critically evaluate selected models of leadership
- consider the models and styles of leadership that are most appropriate to practising professional leadership effectively in social work settings
- examine the skills and attributes required to practise leadership effectively
- reflect upon the relationship between leaders and followers, and leadership and followership
- examine the skills and attributes required to be an effective follower.

Introduction

In the previous chapters we saw how the diverse occupations and activities that broadly make up social work have gradually become more professionalised to the point that social work has now gained the status of a profession. However, we have also seen that, in many people's eyes, social work cannot be regarded in the same way as a 'classic' profession. It has been described variously as a bureau-profession, semi-profession and para-profession. These qualifications to full professionalisation indicate that, while social work has achieved many characteristics of a traditional profession, its practitioners lack both the professional autonomy and professional status enjoyed by members of the more established professions. We have also seen how many commentators have highlighted that social work lacks a strong professional identity which, among other things, means that it has found it difficult to respond to criticisms and also resist the worst excesses of managerialism. At times in its history social work has been said to lack both confidence as a profession and a clear sense of direction and purpose. Uncertainties also remain within social work itself about whether achieving professional status is desirable – for example, in terms of the impact on relationship building with service users and carers.

Regardless of its status as a classic profession or not, social work's many stakeholders, including the general public, expect social workers to be 'professional' in what they do at all times. However, periodically over its history, standards of professionalism have fallen well below acceptable levels in respect of how social work protects those considered to be the most vulnerable in society. Certain high profile tragedies involving social work have led to various reports and policy responses aimed at achieving improvements. In recent years, several important reports have suggested that many of social work's perceived failings could be rectified by better leadership from those in senior management positions. However, more recently, reports have highlighted the need for *all* those involved in social work to demonstrate 'professional leadership' as a means of improving and maintaining standards of professionalism. This has now been embedded in professional capability frameworks.

This brings the spotlight onto what we mean when we talk about leadership. This is another contested and potentially elusive concept. It can mean different things to different people and can take on many forms. Therefore, this chapter begins by exploring different ideas about what leadership is. We examine how concepts of leadership both overlap with and differ from management. We discuss different roles that need to be undertaken for leadership to be effective as well as the skills and attributes needed to be effective in those roles. We then examine selected models of leadership. We focus particularly on collective and situational models, as it is proposed that these approaches might provide the most appropriate basis for considering how professional leadership in social work can be made a meaningful activity.

The chapter then continues by discussing the important interrelationship between leadership and 'followership'. It is argued that understanding what we require from leadership also involves appreciating what is required from followers. However, leaders and followers are not separate people. We all occupy both roles at some point, but at different times. When the situation requires it, leaders need to know when and how to follow and followers need to know when and how to demonstrate a degree of leadership. Leadership and followership are therefore most appropriately regarded as equal but different activities. Attention needs to be paid to how we carry out both roles effectively and how we enable others to do so.

Finally, leadership is a huge topic about which a vast amount has been written over many years in different contexts. What is covered in this chapter is very selective and does not purport to be in any way representative of everything that has been written on this complex and contested subject. There are suggestions for further reading at the end to broaden and deepen your knowledge about leadership. However, if nothing else, a goal of this chapter is to begin to open up different ways of looking at leadership in order to better inform thinking about how professional leadership can be practised meaningfully in everyday social work situations.

Thinking about leaders and leadership

Leadership is a tricky concept to pin down with any great precision. It can mean different things to different people in different contexts. Literally thousands of books have been written on the subject and it is almost impossible to find a definition upon which everyone agrees – even among the experts (Grint, 2010). This means that when calls for leadership are made it cannot be taken for granted that these will be understood by everyone in the same way. However, for the purposes of this chapter we need to come up with some sort of working consensus or else the discussion will not get very far. In this respect it would be useful to mainly confine our thinking to forms of leadership that are likely to be required or practised in the context of work organisations rather than, say, military campaigns or sport. That's not to say that much cannot be transferred from one context to another (and often is), but as the world is awash with definitions and ideas about leadership, it makes sense to filter this down in some way, especially when space is limited. The following activity will hopefully help gather our thoughts towards developing a definition that makes sense and with which we can work.

Activity 3.1   Exploring what is meant by leadership

You are in a meeting at work where it appears that most people are fairly demoralised because, even though everyone is working hard, the organisation isn't performing very well, there are budgetary problems and there are rumours that part of the operation is going to be closed down. As the meeting breaks up a colleague sighs and says, 'I could see this coming, what we need is some proper leadership round here; that's what's been lacking.'

Task

Consider the following questions, and discuss your answers with another if possible.

- Why do you think your colleague made this comment?
- What might they have been expecting from 'proper leadership'?
- Who do you think is or was expected to provide the leadership demanded?
- What thoughts has this stimulated generally about leadership for you?

Commentary

Given the range of different meanings that people attach to leadership it would be understandable if views expressed varied considerably. However, you might have discussed that the appeal for 'proper leadership' was asking for someone (or more than one person) to take control of the situation, solve the financial problems, head off any rumoured closure and generally change things for the better. It appears that the perceived lack of leadership in the past is associated with problems that have mounted up. Your colleague might have been looking for someone to inspire them, to reassure them, to give them a sense of direction and to provide a positive vision for the future so that, among other things, they would want to continue working in that organisation.

Some might have put an emphasis on the leadership needed to sort out the practical problems facing the organisation (a task function) and others might have emphasised more the need to improve the morale of the workforce (a process function). It is not hard to see how both functions link together. However, as to do both effectively requires a range of skills, this suggests that people generally expect leadership to involve a variety of different skills, talents and attributes. This might give a clue as to why quite a lot of people do not see themselves as leaders.

As far as the question goes about *who* they might have in mind to provide the leadership, some might have believed that it was the responsibility of management and that in this scenario the current management would appear not to have provided very effective leadership when it was needed. However, others might have thought that the important point is that the necessary leadership should come from whoever could provide it, especially since the management seemed to have been lacking in this respect. Alternatively, you might have thought that the most effective leadership might have come from managers and others in the organisation pooling their ideas and resources and working collectively.

Hopefully, the activity has started you thinking about leadership. Already a few important points and questions have been raised that can be explored in more detail as the chapter goes on. These include the following suggestions.

- Leadership obviously requires leaders. Often people think that, in a typical work organisation, this will be the management. However, while leadership and management are related in many ways, there are also critical differences.

- Leadership requires a varied skillset and can involve a range of roles and functions. Some functions are more about getting tasks done; others are more about making sure that the group works well together.

- To be effective, leadership requires having an understanding of the bigger picture and how things link together. It is about collective goals rather than personal goals.

- Leadership is associated with creating a sense of direction and helping provide a vision to work towards.

- Leadership involves making sure the right things get done at the appropriate time.

- Leadership involves seeing what changes are needed in any given situation and ensuring that they take place.

- Leadership involves being able to influence others (followers) in positive ways.

Definitions

The activity will have provoked some initial thoughts about what leadership involves and who we think leaders are. Trying to capture the essence of leadership in a sentence or two is challenging. However, below are a series of quotations to further stimulate our thinking on these and other questions.

1. The function of leadership is to produce more leaders, not more followers (Ralph Nader).

2. Leadership is about stepping forward and doing something that otherwise wouldn't be done (Cameron and Green, 2008, p. 6).

3. Leadership is a process whereby an individual influences a group of individuals to achieve a common goal (Northouse, 2015b, p. 6).

The final quotation adds a potentially important qualification to that by Northouse above.

4. Leadership is sometimes defined as 'getting other people to do what you want to do because they want to do it'. I do not agree. If it is your task, why should anyone help you to achieve it? It has to be a common task, one which everyone in the group can share because they see that it has value for the organisation or society and – directly or indirectly – for themselves as well (Adair, 2009a, p. 77).

The first quotation is interesting because it not only draws attention to the role of leadership as an enabling process, but it also recognises that the roles of leader and follower are not fixed. People are seldom just one or the other throughout their lives in every situation they experience. We look more closely at the concept of followership and the relationship between leaders and followers later in this chapter.

The second quotation draws our attention to the fact that leadership involves people being active rather than passive and taking the responsibility to get involved in some way. It suggests that if someone else has not done this, and we can see the need, then we should be the ones to 'step forward'.

The final two quotations draw our attention to the fact that leadership is about a group achieving a 'common goal'. To do that everyone has to be clear what the goal is and be committed to achieving it.

Leadership and management

Many people equate leadership with management and believe that only managers can – and, indeed, should – be the ones to provide leadership. It is quite easy to see why someone would come to this conclusion. For example, in organisations it is a management role to make strategic and operational decisions, managers have the power to tell people what to do and they have the formal responsibility to make sure that everything runs properly. Managers also get paid more money.

However, if we think about our own experiences it is probably not that hard to think of examples where people other than managers (ourselves even) have stepped forward and made suggestions or taken a lead on some area of work either by choice or at the request of others. As MacKian, Russell and McCalla (2013, p. 5) rightly observe, 'someone can be a very effective leader without occupying a management position'. Thinking about the similarities and differences between leadership and management is a useful exercise. This is not just because we do not want to fall into the trap of assuming that, in organisations, only managers provide leadership, but it is also because by considering the differences and similarities we can gain better insights into what leadership involves.

Over the years many have reflected upon the extent to which leadership and management are similar activities, often with differing conclusions. American scholar Warren Bennis was regarded by many as a 'leadership guru'. His book *On becoming a leader* (Bennis, 1994) was regarded as seminal in the business community. Cameron and Green (2008) say that one important point about Bennis was that he made a sharp distinction between managers and leaders. According to Bennis, a leader 'innovates' while a manager 'administers', a leader is 'an original' and a manager 'a copy', a leader is 'his own person' [sic] while a manager is 'the classic good soldier' and so on. In Bennis's view, leaders and managers are very much different animals, with leaders being regarded as having more special talents than managers, who are mainly regarded as cogs in the organisational machine. However, another leadership 'guru' John Adair (2009a, p. 50) believed that 'the truth is that leadership and management are different concepts but they overlap very considerably' – although Adair admitted that how and where they overlap exactly is difficult to determine.

In agreeing with Adair, Northouse (2015b) argued that while it is important to make a distinction between leadership and management, the concepts of leadership and management do sometimes overlap. In characterising a key difference, Northouse elaborated that 'both leadership and management involve influence, but leadership is about seeking constructive change, and management is about establishing order' (ibid., p. 8).

Within social work in England, Skills for Care has developed a Strategy for Leadership and Management Skills (Skills for Care, 2008), which suggests there is a continuum from leadership to management with an overlap of common activities. Lawler and Bilson (2010, p. 36) produced such a continuum of their own. At the leadership end they identify activities such as 'inspiration', 'transformation', 'creativity', 'innovation'; and 'motivation'. 'Common areas' between leadership and management include 'communication', 'negotiation' and 'decision making'; at the strictly management end they include activities such as 'delegation', 'planning', 'monitoring and evaluating' and 'formal supervision'. Even though one can always debate exactly where an activity might be located on such a continuum, it is a useful way of separating out these two often conflated sets of activities. Management activities tend to be more routinised, dealing with largely predictable situations; leadership concerns itself more with new problems and situations. This fits in with the analysis put forward by Grint (2010). He says that management tends to be about dealing with previously experienced problems ('tame problems'), whereas leadership is about the need to innovate to solve problems that are novel, open-ended and multi-factoral ('wicked problems'). We discuss the concept of 'wicked problems' in greater length later in the chapter in relation to collective and situational models of leadership.

The sheer weight of literature on the subject indicates that it is hard to settle on any definitive conclusions. However, in the context of this chapter, one of the main points to highlight is that, despite overlaps, leadership and management should not be regarded as the same thing and, more importantly for the purpose of this book generally, that leadership need neither be the sole preserve nor the sole responsibility of managers. Within organisations, there are many potential leadership roles that can be played by just about anyone if and when the situation calls for it. Whether this be organising the Christmas party or a colleague's leaving gift, we can all probably think of such examples. Many leadership roles, such as making insightful suggestions, asking clarifying questions, problem-solving and motivating others, do not have to be exclusively taken on by managers. To return to the point made earlier by Northouse, a key feature of leadership is about seeking constructive change. Anyone can play a part in this.

Leadership roles

The discussion above has alerted us to the fact that leadership involves a range of roles, some more task-focused, others more process- or group-focused. We have established that while many are undertaken by managers, not all are. In this section we reflect more upon the different roles played by leaders.

Activity 3.2

Drawing on the discussion above but also bringing in your own ideas, make a list of all the possible roles that you think come under the heading of leadership.

Commentary

Most lists would probably have included: inspiring, innovating, providing direction, asking 'why' questions, challenging the status quo, transforming, doing what you consider is 'the right thing', motivating, establishing a vision, communicating the vision/direction, role-modelling, producing change and empowering people. All of these underline not only that there are many roles required in leadership, but also that it is unlikely that all can be performed effectively by just one person or a small number of select individuals in an organisation. This suggests that often people are happier playing to their strengths in this respect. It is therefore useful for all of us not only to have sense of our strengths, but also our weaknesses (or areas for development, if you prefer).

Belbin roles

Cameron and Green (2008) propose that a good starting point for looking at what different people can bring to leadership roles is to use the framework of 'team roles' devised by Meredith Belbin (1981). Belbin argued that there were eight/nine roles that need to be undertaken if teams are to work effectively together and get the results they want. They are:

1. The Coordinator (Chairman) provides leadership by coordinating the efforts and contributions of the team members.

2. The Shaper (Driver) provides leadership by directing and controlling team members.

3. The Completer (Finisher) is the type of person who pays close attention to detail and follows up on unfinished tasks.

4. The Implementer (Company Worker) is good at accomplishing detailed and practical outcomes.

5. The Monitor-Evaluator is good at evaluating ideas and suggestions.

6. The Plant (Originator) is the 'ideas person' of the team. They are good at generating ideas to deal with problems confronting the team.

7. The Resource Investigator acts as a source of information and ideas.

8. The Team Worker (Supporter) helps to maintain group harmony and team spirit.

9. The Specialist provides knowledge or skills that are in rare supply. They are not always needed on every occasion.

On the Belbin website (http://www.belbin.com/about/belbin-team-roles/) it explains that most people have two or three roles that they are most comfortable with and offers a questionnaire for people to self-assess where their particular tendencies and strengths lie. There are no 'good' or 'bad' team roles. Each team role has its strengths and weaknesses, and each has equal importance. However, not all are required at the same time. It is possible to see how some of the roles are more obviously what we might regard as leader roles and others follower roles. However, the interesting point is that the team will usually not function effectively unless all the roles are covered in some way, underlining the important relationship between leadership and (active) followership, which we will explore in more depth later.

Case study 3.1   The student network

Alish, Mandeep and Aaron are students on a Step Up to Social Work course. They have all just started placements at different teams in the local Children and Families Social Care department. When Alish discovers that there are already four other social work students from different courses placed in the same organisation she has the idea that they should form a student

→

network to exchange information and offer peer support and supervision. Mandeep convenes a meeting of all seven students and the idea receives a positive response. Patience (a BA student) offers to set up a Facebook and WhatsApp group to facilitate communication. Aaron says he has some ideas for guest speakers and offers to contact them. Bobby (an MA student) says that he will do the 'admin' – that is to say, keep records, maintain the diary of events and meetings and generally make sure that everyone's role is clear and efforts are well coordinated. As he said, only half joking, 'This will all make for good evidence for the professional leadership domain.'

Pleased with the way that her idea has been adopted, Alish decides to see if she can link the network to any other social work student networks in the region. Joella (a BA student) says that if Alish is successful she will use her baking skills to host a social event.

With the network beginning to take shape, Rory (an MA student) offers to write up their experiences and send in an article to *Community Care* magazine. Bobby offers to gather the thoughts of everyone involved and help with proofreading and editing. Rory's only problem was that he could not think of a title for his article.

Cameron and Green's five roles

From lengthy studies on the various roles that leaders play, Cameron and Green (2008) distilled this down to 'five roles used by effective leaders'. They are:

1. **Edgy catalyser**

   o   asks the difficult, penetrating questions;
   o   spots dysfunction and resistance;
   o   creates discomfort and unease when things aren't improving.

2. **Visionary motivator**

   o   articulates a compelling picture of the future;
   o   energises groups of people and engages them;
   o   holds the vision long enough and strong enough for others to step into.

3. **Measured connector**

   o   reinforces what's important and establishes a few simple rules;
   o   calmly influences complex change activity through focused reassurance;
   o   connects people and agendas.

4. **Tenacious implementer**

   o   doggedly pursues the plan;
   o   holds people to account;
   o   leads by driving a project through to completion.

5. **Thoughtful architect**

o is principal architect and designer of the strategies; crafts seemingly disparate ideas into a way forward;

o scans the environment, sees what's happening in the environment and creates an organising framework.

Adapted from Cameron and Green (2008, Chapter 3)

Cameron and Green's approach reflects the move away from 'great man' or 'heroic leader' theories of leadership which focus on special innate qualities that only 'natural' leaders are supposed to possess – such as charisma. Rather, they acknowledge that because we are all different in terms of factors such as our personality, background, education and life experiences we probably fit more easily into some of the roles than we do others. However, they stress the desirability of extending our repertoire by 'playing around a little' with the roles that we could step into or perhaps the roles we choose to step into. None of us comes ready-made with all the skills and qualities needed to play all the roles. We discover what we can do and what we are good at through the experiences we have. Often people who do not consider themselves as leaders find that they can manage to rise to the occasion when it demands it.

Among the leadership literature, many authors over the years have produced their own lists of roles and behaviours that they believe are necessary for effective leadership. What most such lists have in common is that they are based on an approach to leadership which (as was highlighted earlier) focuses on two types of behaviour: *task* behaviours (getting the job done) and *process* behaviours (ensuring that the work group is functioning well). Although this approach to leadership has been around since at least the 1930s and 1940s (Northouse, 2015b), it still has a lot of appeal because it confirms the point that, to be effective, leadership requires a range of different behaviours and, as with Belbin's approach to team roles, it allows for different people to play leadership roles according to their strengths. It does not assume that a single 'heroic' leader or small group of leaders should or can do everything. That said, the 'behavioural' approach to leadership has been criticised for not focusing enough on the relationship between leaders and followers and not paying sufficient attention to the roles that followers play as part of an overall collective effort in achieving common goals. These are points we address later in the chapter.

The 'incomplete leader' and 'sense-making'

The fact that a single leader cannot meet all the challenges of leadership is taken up by Ancona et al. (2007), who develop the idea of the 'incomplete leader'. They argue that, in a world where the problems that we face are increasingly complex, no single person can embody all the qualities of the complete leader and perform all the necessary roles adequately. In fact, they suggest that leaders who try will only exhaust themselves and endanger the organisations for which they work. They regard leadership as a collective effort based upon four leadership capabilities that all organisations need. They are:

- sense-making – making sense of the world around us/interpreting developments;
- relating – building trusting relationships;
- visioning – communicating a compelling image of the future;
- inventing – coming up with new ways of doing things.

Sense-making

While most people might think that 'relating', 'visioning' and 'inventing' are key leadership capabilities, they might not automatically add 'sense-making' to the list. However, in an ever-changing and complex environment, whether it be social work, business or any other line of activity, being able to understand the context of what is going on, to make sense of what is happening and also getting a sense of what might be coming down the line in the future is of vital importance. It would be hard to lead in other respects if sense-making did not take place. Smircich and Morgan (1982, p. 259) have described leadership as 'a process of defining reality in ways that are sensible to the led'. Potentially, being able to establish a shared 'reality' in ways that others can fully grasp and use as a reference point to follow and guide their actions is one of the most important leadership capabilities. Arguably, it is one that is difficult to undertake alone. If reality is to be socially constructed it requires collaboration with others. According to Grint (2005), leadership should be thought of as the 'consequence of sense-making activities by organizational members.' He adds:

> *That is not to say that sense-making is a democratic activity because there are always some people more involved in sense-making than others and these 'leaders' are those 'bricoleurs' – people who make sense from variegated materials that they are faced with, and manage to construct a novel solution to a specific problem from this assembly of materials.*

Ibid., p. 39

Grint's analysis is interesting, not only because it introduces the thought-provoking concept of the leader as 'bricoleur' to the discussion, but also because he makes the point that there are 'some people more involved in sense-making than others'. Nevertheless, sense-making is still best seen as a collective activity. It is most likely to take place when leaders are not only engaged in 'sense-making' dialogues with other leaders, but also with followers who, at the very least, are prepared to act as sounding boards. At this point it is worth pointing out the distinction some make between 'sense-making' and 'sense-giving'. It is argued that whereas the former is largely about meaning-making and interpretation, the latter activity is about the process of actively influencing others to accept your preferred definition of reality (Gioia and Chittipeddi, 1991). We therefore need to be aware that what might appear to be mutual sense-making might involve at least an element of one party trying to force their views on others. This further underlines the importance of focusing on the leader–follower relationship and the roles that followers can play.

The thrust of this chapter so far has been to argue that leadership in organisations should best be regarded as a collective endeavour shared among many people. As we shall see, this is not necessarily a view that everyone would support, but given that it is currently common for models of collective leadership to be advocated across the public sector, it would be beneficial to pay closer attention to the rationale provided for collective models and how they are supposed to work.

The King's Fund is an influential health and care charity which commissioned a series of reports into the leadership of health and social care for the Commission on Leadership and Management in the NHS (see, Hartley and Bennington, 2011; Turnbull James, 2011; West et al., 2014). The activity below uses extracts from one of the reports as a means of exploring the thinking behind collective leadership and why it has become so popular in the public sector.

Models of leadership: Collective, distributed and situational

Activity 3.3

1. Read the following extracts from *Developing collective leadership for health care* (West et al., 2014).
2. Answer the questions at the end.
3. Discuss your answers with another if possible.

The NHS needs leadership of the highest calibre if it is to respond successfully to financial and service pressures that are unprecedented in its history. In previous reports, the King's Fund has argued that we need to move on from a concept of heroic leaders who turn around organisational performance to seeing leadership as shared and distributed throughout the NHS. The Fund has also argued that leaders must engage their colleagues and other stakeholders in bringing about improvements in patient care and transforming the way in which care is provided (ibid., p. 2).

Collective leadership means everyone taking responsibility for the success of the organisation as a whole – not just for their own jobs or work area. This contrasts with traditional approaches to leadership, which have focused on developing individual capability while neglecting the need for developing collective capability or embedding the development of leaders within the context of the organisation they are working in (ibid., p. 4).

A collective leadership strategy emerges from a conscious and intelligent effort to plan for an integrated, collective network of leaders, including patients, distributed throughout the organisation and embodying shared values and practices (Browning, Torain and Patterson, 2011; Hartley and Bennington, 2011). The aim of the strategy must be to create a leadership community in which all staff take responsibility for nurturing cultures of high quality and compassionate care. The strategy should require all staff to prioritise the effectiveness of the organisation and sector as a whole in creating this culture, rather than focusing only on individual or team success. Every member of staff has the potential to lead at many points in time, particularly when their expertise is relevant to the task in hand. It is also important to ensure all staff are focused on good followership, regardless of their seniority in the organisation. To achieve this, senior leaders must understand the leadership practices and behaviours needed to nurture a caring culture. Understanding culture alone is insufficient; conscious, deliberate attention must be paid to enabling people at every level within the organisation to adopt leadership practices that nurture the cultures the NHS requires. For collective, distributed leadership (and followership), all staff must be engaged (West et al., 2014, p. 8).

Leadership comes from both the leaders themselves and the relationships among them. Organisational performance does not rest simply on the number or quality of individual leaders. What counts is the extent to which formal and informal leaders work collectively in support of the organisation's goals and in embodying the values that underpin the desired culture. Leadership also incorporates the concept of followership – everyone supporting each other, including leaders, to deliver high quality care, and everyone taking responsibility for the success of the organisation as a whole (ibid., p. 14).

Activity 3.4

1. What is the rationale provided for collective leadership in the NHS?
2. What model of leadership is it supposed to replace?
3. Identify key phrases from the extracts that help you understand the principles of collective leadership.
4. In what ways is 'followership' considered important?
5. Do you have any critical thoughts about the proposed model, either in theory or how it might pan out in practice?

Commentary

Clearly, one would need to read the whole document to fully understand all the fine grain of what is entailed. However, the extracts provide strong clues as to the rationale for advocating collective leadership. Collective leadership is seen, among other things, as a means of achieving important goals for the NHS. They include transforming the way care is provided; nurturing 'high quality and compassionate care' and responding successfully to 'unprecedented financial and service pressures'.

The King's Fund says that they want to move on from 'traditional approaches to leadership which focused on individual capability'. They are therefore turning away from individual 'heroic' leadership. It is not said in the extracts but, implicitly, the King's Fund appears to have lost faith in the model of 'transformational leadership' that became popular in the public sector following its emergence in the 1980s. This approach largely relied on charismatic, visionary and inspirational individuals (sometimes known as 'change agents') to motivate followers (i.e. the rest of the work force) to identify with the leader and his or her values; buy into their vision; and to work towards their common goals (Northouse, 2015b).

You could have identified several key phrases that provide an insight into the principle of collective leadership as expounded by the King's Fund. For example, they state that (with my emphasis added in italics):

- Collective leadership means *everyone taking responsibility for the success of the organisation as a whole* . . .

- The aim of the strategy must be *to create a leadership community in which all staff take responsibility for nurturing cultures* of high quality and compassionate care.

- . . . *conscious, deliberate attention must be paid to enabling people at every level within the organisation to adopt leadership practices that nurture the cultures* the NHS requires.

- Leadership comes from both the leaders themselves *and the relationships among them.*

- *What counts is the extent to which formal and informal leaders work collectively* in support of the organisation's goals and in embodying the values that underpin the *desired culture.*

- *Every member of staff has the potential to lead at many points in time, particularly when their expertise is relevant to the task in hand.*

- *Leadership also incorporates the concept of followership – everyone supporting each other* . . . (West et al., 2014, pp. 4, 8, 14)

In summary, collective leadership involves all staff, at every level, taking responsibility for achieving organisational success. It involves everyone actively working towards building a leadership 'community' that can nurture the required organisational culture. This necessarily requires the involvement of formal and informal leaders (that is to say, those in formal management roles and those who are leaders by experience) working together.

However, the King's Fund says that collective leadership involves a mutually supportive relationship between leadership and followership. This model is about creating what Raelin (2003) has called 'leaderful organisations'. This is where leadership can come from everyone in the organisation working collaboratively for a common purpose rather than as the result of the influence of individuals in powerful positions. In leaderful organisations followers become leaders and vice versa, as required.

Situational leadership

The approach to leadership proposed by the King's Fund is collective but also 'situational'. What this means is that it is expected to utilise whichever style of leadership is most effective at that time, from whoever has the expertise to respond to the situational requirements at the time (Bolden et al., 2003; Adair, 2009b). Adair (2009b, p. 13) proposes that with the situational approach, 'you need not have an appointed or elected leader in a group – just let the situation decide who should be the leader!'. The situational model therefore regards leadership and leadership styles as both *emergent* (i.e. coming into a being at a particular time) and *contingent* on what particular situation has arisen.

As far as critical thoughts about collective leadership go, many would still regard leadership as something that must necessarily come from the top downwards or, at least, from a few select individuals in positions of power. The reasoning would be that any attempt to spread leadership among too many people risks confusion, chaos and even anarchy – 'too many cooks', as the saying goes. We can all probably think of situations where too many leaders or potential leaders pulling in different directions have hindered rather than helped problem-solving and task completion. There are certainly many examples from politics to back this up. Another criticism that some have made is that telling everyone that leadership is their responsibility can sound a bit like managers wanting to deflect what, ultimately, should be their responsibility onto others. They are paid to take the difficult decisions. The counter argument to this is that organisations where there is a clear demarcation between 'us' (the workers) and 'them' (the bosses) are more likely to become adversarial, less likely to prosper, adapt and survive in challenging and competitive times. Therefore, the well-being of the organisation must be everyone's responsibility, goes the argument. The challenges are too complex and changeable for the workforce to simply say 'it's not our problem' and refuse to engage with the challenges of leadership. Therefore, for this, and other reasons, collective and situational approaches to leadership have been proposed as a logical way forward for the public sector to deal with its many challenges. However, as we have highlighted, while there are benefits claimed, there are also challenges involved in making these approaches work in practice. Next we examine these in more detail.

The benefits and challenges of collective models of leadership

For the purposes of this discussion 'collective' is used as an umbrella term to talk about forms of 'dispersed', 'distributed', 'democratic' and 'shared' models of leadership. However, it is acknowledged that while they are often used interchangeably, there are nuances of difference between the way these terms are used at times (Schedlitzki and Edwards, 2014). They are, nevertheless, in the same family and sit in opposition to traditional individual models.

Benefits

The King's Fund states that 'collective leadership entails distributing and allocating leadership power to wherever expertise, capability and motivation sit within organisations' (West et al., 2014, p. 7). Therefore, this approach represents a move away from a command and control/top down (vertical) model of leadership power to something where power is exercised in a more democratic and dispersed (horizontal) fashion (Turnbull James, 2011). It can be understood as a kind of 'we're all in this together' approach designed to utilise everybody's various talents for the common good. However, this does raise a few difficult questions, not least of which are: how does the distribution and allocation of leadership power take place and how is it ensured that – to use the phrase again – too many cooks do not spoil the broth in the process? How is collective leadership coordinated so that everyone is pulling in the same direction? Does it happen spontaneously or does it require direction from senior leaders?

The concept of distribution refers to the idea that leadership skills and responsibilities are dispersed throughout the organisation. Advocates of the model argue that, first and foremost, for distributed leadership to work, everyone needs to be clear about what the collective goals are. For this to happen everyone needs to communicate with each other and, at some point, participate in the sense-making process. According to Gronn (2002) distributed leadership can vary in how spontaneously it happens. It can involve spontaneous collaboration when groups of individuals with differing skills, knowledge and/or capabilities come together to complete a particular task/project and then disband. When it is less spontaneous it requires the creation of a community culture that inspires, shapes and sustains leadership practice geared to achieving the collective goals. Senior managers might play a part in creating such a culture but they cannot do it on their own. It requires both formal and informal leaders *and* followers involved collectively in making sense of what the challenges are, what the goals are and what should be done to achieve them. A consequence of this is that different leaders emerge to perform the necessary task and group maintenance focused activities (see Figure 3.1).

Gronn (ibid.) highlights two other ways in which distributed leadership can occur. It can be the result of intuitive working between colleagues in teams which develops over time or it can develop through institutionalised practices where 'enduring organisational structures', such as committees, teams or networking meetings, are implemented in order to facilitate collaboration between individuals. A critical point is that, whether it happens spontaneously or not, distributed leadership emerges *outside* an organisation's formal management hierarchy. It does not solely come from the top down neither does it depend on formal positional power. Leadership functions are undertaken by people regardless of their formal role in the organisation. Brookes and Grint (2010, p. 8) define shared leadership as 'how we lead when we are not in charge'.

Research into the distributed model in operation in a high tech organisation showed an increase in both creativity and productivity (Politis, 2005). Fig 3.1 [based on Lawler and Bilson (2010, p. 68)] sets out key distributed leadership functions together with the knowledge and skills associated with these functions. Note how they are grouped under 'task' and 'maintenance' functions and are therefore similar to Belbin's team roles in many respects. Nearly all of them can be undertaken by anybody regardless of their formal position in the organisational hierarchy.

Challenges

Hierarchical organisations

Writers such as Lumby (2016) and Currie and Lockett (2011) have highlighted that one of the obvious problems with the distributed leadership model is that it runs into difficulties when tried in hierarchical, managerialised bureaucratic organisations which,

Task functions	(Group) maintenance functions
Information and opinion giver	Participation encourager
Information and opinion seeker	Harmoniser and compromiser
Starter	Tension reliever
Direction giver	Process observer
Energiser	Inter-personal problem-solver
Reality tester	Evaluator of emotional climate
Diagnoser	Active listener
Coordinator	Trust builder
Required	**Required**
Subject/discipline knowledge	Knowledge of group behaviour/dynamics
Process skills	People skills

Figure 3.1   Key distributed leadership functions

Source: Adapted from Lawler and Bilson, 2010

it so happens, most public sector organisations are – whether this be in education, health or social care. Opportunities to practise spontaneously or intuitively in such environments are severely curtailed.

Lack of a solid evidence base

Outside education (and even here the evidence is mixed (Lumby, 2016)), models of distributed or collective leadership might be confident about what they can achieve in theory but, as with situational leadership theory, they lack a solid evidence base in practice (Schedlitzki and Edwards, 2014). Lumby (2016) argues that while the idea of distributed leadership has become fashionable in recent years, in practice, it has often become diluted and 'hybridised' to the point that even conventional top down models with little discernible collaborative activity or power sharing call themselves 'distributed'. Therefore, 'pure' distributed leadership is so hard to find in practice that it is impossible to know whether it is effective or not.

Linking collective and situational models to professional leadership in social work

We have briefly reviewed some of the benefits and challenges associated with models of collective and situational leadership in the context of work organisations. However, the overall focus of this book is *professional leadership in social work.* This will obviously take place within organisations much of the time but will also take place between and outside organisations as well. Nevertheless, it is proposed that collective and situational models of leadership provide the best overall fit for how professional leadership in social work should be approached. One reason for this is that social work largely takes place in different public sector organisations working to multiple agendas involving a diverse range of stakeholders. Many of the problems with which social work is engaged could be described as 'wicked problems' (Rittel and Webber, 1973). These are problems such as those associated with social deprivation, which have multiple causes and are impossible to solve by just taking one course of action. Wicked problems not only have complex origins, they also emerge in a context where there are contradictory opinions about what to do, incomplete information upon which to base solutions and changing ideas about what outcomes are required. Expecting a few powerful leaders, however expert or charismatic, to solve these problems is asking a lot. The extent and nature of the task suggests it would benefit from collaborative effort and the pooling of expertise.

A second reason for choosing collective and situational models is because, as we saw in Chapter 2, professional guidance states that all social workers (and social work students) at every level need to demonstrate some degree of professional leadership appropriate to their level and role.

It is a requirement of registration. This strongly suggests that professional leadership in social work is regarded primarily both as a collective and situational activity. That is not to say that aspects of other models might be not applicable. Therefore, suggestions for further reading are provided at the end of this chapter for readers who want to explore all aspects of leadership more fully.

Whatever model is adopted to inform our approach to professional leadership in social work, we need to ask a few pertinent questions, such as 'What do we actually want and expect from such leadership?' For example, do we want others to tell us what to do? 'How do we do leadership in a way that is most likely to achieve our goals *and* reflect social work values?' 'What approach to leadership will most likely enhance standards of professionalism and raise the standing of social work as a profession?'

With these questions in mind, we end this section with some thoughts from Grint (2010, p. 126), who proposes that, in reality, the leadership task is both an individual and a collective one.

> *We cannot achieve coordinated responses to collective wicked problems simply by turning our backs upon individual leadership – even collaborative leadership requires individuals to make the first move, to assume responsibility, and to mobilize the collective leadership. In effect, the members of the collective must authorize each other to lead because collectives are notoriously poor at decision-making. Leadership is not, then, the elephant in the room that many would rather not face up to; it is the room itself – which we cannot do without. This, in another world, is what Bauman calls, 'the unbearable silence of responsibility'. And this is our collective and individual challenge.*

Given that professionalism means taking responsibility for one's self, one's own well-being and one's own work as well as that of our colleagues, all of those involved in social work need to reflect on how best to manage the professional leadership challenges they face both as individuals and as part of a bigger collective body of people.

The skills and attributes required to practise leadership effectively

We have seen how leadership studies have moved away from simply focusing on models that are interested in the special attributes and skills required by a few at the top of organisations. We have highlighted the emergence of models that see leadership practice as necessarily dispersed, distributed, collective and situational. It has been recognised that leadership need not require special or innate qualities. Leadership skills can be learned and leadership attributes developed through training and experience. Therefore, in this section, we focus on the range of leadership skills and attributes that an organisation needs to have among its workforce in order for it to be successful in achieving its goals.

Leadership skills

Earlier in the chapter, one of the selected definitions of leadership explained it was where an 'individual influences a group of individuals to achieve a common goal' (Northouse, 2015b, p. 6). This quotation reflects the commonly held view that to be able to influence others in some way or another is critical in leadership. We used the ideas of both Belbin, and Cameron and Green to stimulate thinking about the range of roles that are needed for leadership to be effective, especially when viewed as a collective, distributed and shared activity.

The following activity is designed to encourage you to think about the range of skills needed to undertake these different roles and functions. It will underline how extremely unlikely it is that any one person could possibly possess all these skills, but it should also highlight that everyone can contribute something.

Activity 3.5   Leadership: Skills and attributes

As a starting assumption let us say that, overall, leadership is about influencing people to achieve common goals. Figure 3.1 lists distributed leadership functions under two broad headings which have been highlighted throughout this chapter – task and maintenance functions – the assumption being that any group needs to attend equally to both of these functions if it wants to achieve its goals.

Task

1. Reflect upon Figure 3.1 and think more about what the two sets of functions involve. Make a list of the various skills and attributes that you believe are needed to effectively cover the two functions set out.
2. From the list you have produced, what do you think your own particular strengths are? Where do you need to develop?

Commentary

Everyone's list of skills and attributes will differ. However, to stimulate discussion, a suggested list of skills and attributes has been sub-categorised under the broad headings: 'interpersonal', 'emotional', 'cognitive/intellectual' and 'technical' below. Different headings could have been used, some skills could have been listed under more than one heading and there are often overlaps between the different skills and attributes.

Interpersonal

- Communication
- Clearly expressing one's ideas and thoughts
- Listening
- Persuasion
- Ability to have challenging conversations
- Asking 'why' and 'how' questions constructively
- Good at explanation
- Humour
- Able to give and receive constructive criticism
- Able to construct an argument
- Provide a good role model

Emotional

- Emotional intelligence
- Attention to the needs and feelings of others
- Honest/genuine
- Trustworthy
- Observant
- Sensitive to one's own mood and the moods of others
- Resilient
- Reflexive
- Mindful
- Ability to express and manage emotions
- Assertive
- Comfortable with authority

Cognitive/intellectual

- Curiosity
- Open-minded
- Research
- Problem-solving
- Hypothesis
- Analysis
- Critical thinker
- Creativity/generate news, ideas
- Develop ideas
- Can use initiative

Technical

- Understand both the wider and the specific contexts in which decisions and tasks take place
- Be able to understand the specific requirements of the law, policy and other technical guidelines
- Attention to detail
- Understand and decode specialist language
- Ability to keep things on track and stay focused on the task
- Be able to coach or educate others using specific methods

Commentary

The list of skills and attributes is almost certainly not exhaustive and in many cases you could dispute which skills went under which heading or whether one was the same as another listed elsewhere. However, what emerges from this exercise is, first, that the range of skills and attributes required in being a leader is wide and diverse (confirming the point made by Ancona et al. that no one has all of these); second, that we will excel in some areas more than others; third, that just about all of these skills and attributes can be developed with practice; and, lastly, that mostly they are about how we use our self in relationships with others. Therefore, having a critical awareness of self, the ability to communicate and the ability to build and manage relationships are all fundamental leadership skills. They also happen to be fundamental social work skills and we will return to how we can develop our skills and attributes in the context of professional leadership in social work in Chapter 5. However, we next turn our attention to examining the relationship between leaders and followers.

The relationship between leadership and followership

Traditional studies of leadership tended to ignore the relationships between leaders and followers (Roe, 2017). However, the leader–follower relationship, and followership generally, were brought to prominence by Kelley's article 'In praise of followers' in the *Harvard Business Review* (1988). Since then it has become more widely recognised that to omit consideration of the role played by followers is missing an important dimension of leadership.

Whether it be in the context of leadership studies or in popular discourse, Grint (2005, 2010) points out that, typically, representations of followers generally have negative connotations. Followers are either invisible cyphers or are constructed as passive disciples and unthinking 'sheep', following in the wake of their leader or waiting to be told what to do. However, while some of that description might be applicable in some instances, such representations misrepresent the complexity and diversity of relationships that can occur between leaders and followers. The following activity will begin to tease out some of these complexities.

Activity 3.6   The leader has got us lost

Try to remember a situation where, as a family group or group of friends, you went on a trip to a new country or new part of the country. Often on such occasions one or two people – either through their position, age or some other factor – assume the leadership of the group. Therefore, if the group decides to go on an excursion – walking, cycling, boating, driving or by public transport – the leader takes control of the map, compass, satnav, steering controls, train timetable or whatever, and literally leads from the front. The group goes where they go, basically.

(Continued)

(Continued)

Task

1. Imagine you are one of the 'followers' of the group. Now try to remember an occasion where the leader didn't really know what they were doing or where they were going. They got the group lost. What happened? If you managed to get to your destination, how did you manage it? What roles did the so-called 'followers' play?
2. Share your stories and experiences in a small group.

Commentary

It would be surprising if you could not summon up an example that broadly fits the scenario above. Such situations are not that uncommon. Hopefully, it was not too painful or traumatic to recall, but often such episodes end up being the source of humorous anecdotes.

What you probably found was that a variety of follower behaviours occur in those circumstances, some more constructive than others. Sometimes there is a direct swap where the person who was the leader passes control to another member of the group with varying degrees of reluctance. Often followers start to communicate their concerns at stages along the way, asking questions such as: 'Are you sure this is the way we should be going?'; 'Were we supposed to be going to the temple, because I'm sure I saw a sign to it about half a mile back there?'; 'Are you sure you actually know how to read Spanish/read a map?' and so on. In these situations the leaders retain notional control but receive varying degrees of input and support from the followers of group. Sometimes these communications help get the party back on track, at other times they simply serve to question the leader's leadership credentials and stoke levels of discontent within the group. Sometimes followers within the group express doubts to each other but do not communicate these with the leader for various reasons. After finally reaching your destination, someone might say, 'We'd have got here a lot quicker if we had taken the sign when we first left the town.' 'Why didn't you say that at the time?' asks the leader. 'You didn't ask,' replies the follower. Sometimes someone will reply, disingenuously, 'You were the leader, I assumed you knew what you were doing.' Lastly, if the experience proves to be too difficult, another common response is for a follower to announce accusingly, but belatedly, 'I thought the whole idea was stupid and was never going to work in the first place. If we'd have gone to the beach as I was thinking, we'd not have wasted the day.'

There are many variations on these themes. They provide fascinating examples of group dynamics. Followers can be active, passive, constructive and destructive in how they relate to leaders. Even the example provided illustrates the diverse and complicated ways in which leaders and followers can relate to each other. Some ways help the group move forward to where they want to go, but others do not.

The leader–follower relationship

One important point to the activity was to underline that, throughout our lives, we find ourselves either in the role of leader or follower on numerous diverse occasions. We know from experience that the two roles are inextricably linked. It was also making the point that things do not always work out well between leaders and followers. How leaders and followers relate to each other is usually critical in how well the group achieves its goals. Just as effective leadership doesn't come naturally as a gift or happen automatically because of someone's designated position, neither does effective followership. We could all probably testify to the fact that a good leader–follower relationship does not come automatically either. Kelley (1988, p. 142) makes this interesting point:

> Bosses are not necessarily good leaders; subordinates are not necessarily effective followers. Many bosses couldn't lead a horse to water. Many subordinates couldn't follow a parade. Some people avoid either role. Others accept the role thrust upon them and perform it badly.

> At different points in their careers, even at different times of the working day, most managers play both roles, though seldom equally well. After all, the leadership role has the glamour and attention. We take courses to learn it, and when we play it well we get applause and recognition.

Kelley highlights the key point that, despite the fact that leadership traditionally has more kudos attached to it than followership, effective leadership can only happen if there is effective followership. Leaders cannot operate in isolation from followers. In fact, Kelley argues that we should leave aside stereotyped ideas about seeing the leadership role as superior to that of the follower and, instead, we should think of them as *equal but different* activities (my italics).

The importance of achieving an effective relationship between leaders and followers is made all the more critical when you consider that, in a collective approach, roles are fluid. Someone leading on one aspect of work could be a follower on another and vice versa. Given the potential fluidity of the roles, it is clearly in everyone's mutual interest to ensure that respect and cooperation are reciprocated. However, as the activity illustrated, for a variety of reasons leader–follower relationships can be complicated and are as likely to be destructive (or at least dysfunctional) as they are constructive. Since Kelley first wrote on the subject, attention has increasingly come to be focused on relationship approaches to leadership which means examining the nature of followership more closely. Schedlitzki and Edwards (2014) charted the evolution in what they call 'follower-centric' approaches to leadership. The evolution starts with an approach towards followers as merely passive recipients of leadership and sees thinking gradually change until followers are seen as 'co-producers' of leadership. In this conceptualisation the leader–follower relationship is seen as socially co-constructed by leader and follower.

This underlines the fact that leaders and followers are not different people. As Kelley (1988) has pointed out, followers and leaders are often the same people playing different parts at different hours of the day. Seen in this way the relationship between leadership and follow-ership is not necessarily uni-directional and linear, it is a complex and dynamic interactive process. Therefore, an important point to establish is that ideas about what makes for effective leadership have largely ceased to focus solely on the qualities and behaviours of leaders and widened their scope to recognise the importance of understanding how effective leader–follower relationships operate.

If we return to the issue of how professional leadership in social work can be put into practice, the main points to highlight from this discussion are that:

- there is no sharp distinction between those who lead and those who follow (they are not different people);
- that leadership and followership roles vary and can be reversed;
- that followers can behave in ways that involve aspects of leadership; and
- that followers can behave in a variety of ways that either enable or disable leadership.

Two relevant concepts that Grint (2010) discusses are useful to introduce in this context. They are:

- *Constructive dissent*: a form of follower dissent intended to protect the collective and prevent leaders from taking erroneous decisions.
- *Destructive assent*: a form of follower assent that threatens the collective by acquiescing to an erroneous decision by its leaders.

Ibid., pp. 133–4

Before we examine follower behaviours more closely, from either the leader's or follower's perspective, think about examples of when you have experienced constructive dissent and destructive assent. Think about times when your or others' follower behaviour has either pro-tected or threatened the collective. Bear these in mind for the next activity.

The skills and attributes required to be an effective follower

We have established that leaders and followers are not different species of people. As Kelley (1988) argued, followership is not a person but a role that we take on in certain situations and in certain contexts. A leader at one time of the day can be a follower the next. A follower on one subject can be a leader in another. Therefore, as Kelley acknowledges, the qualities that make effective followers are more or less the same qualities found in effective leaders. Again, as with effective leadership, one would not expect one person to embody all the skills and qualities required for effective followership. However, one would hope that they were distributed among the team. Ideally, leaders and followers combined should possess task- and process-focused capabilities. But, as Activity 3.5 highlighted, this is not always the case. Some followers are more effective in protecting the collective than others. Some followers, either consciously or unconsciously, can effectively disable the leader and prevent the team from achieving its goals. We have looked at which leader behaviours are effective; it is only logical to turn our attention to follower behaviours. In his analysis of why some followers are more effective than others, Kelley (ibid.) identifies five followership patterns in which followers vary to the extent that they are either passive or active, independent or dependent, critical or uncritical thinkers. They are:

Sheep are passive and uncritical, lacking in initiative and sense of responsibility. They perform the tasks given them and stop.

Yes People are a livelier but equally unenterprising group. Dependent on a leader for inspiration, they can be aggressively deferential, even servile. Bosses weak in judgement and self-confidence tend to like them and to form alliances with them that can stultify the organisation.

Alienated Followers are critical and independent in their thinking but passive in carrying out their role. Somehow, sometime, something turned them off. Often cynical, they tend to sink gradually into disgruntled acquiescence, seldom openly opposing a leader's efforts.

Survivors perpetually sample the wind and live by the slogan 'better safe than sorry'. They are adept at surviving change.

Effective Followers think for themselves and carry out their duties and assignments with energy and assertiveness. Because they are risk takers, self-starters and independent problem-solvers, they get consistently high ratings from peers and many superiors.

In many ways the five types of follower should be seen as ideal types. In reality, most group members do not exhibit the same behaviours or adopt the same role all the time. It is important not to pigeonhole and 'fix' followers any more than it is leaders. Factors such as organisational context, timing, group dynamics and leadership style need to be taken into account in how roles come to be adopted. However, Kelley's grid provides a useful way for us to reflect on the impact that different types of follower behaviour can have.

Activity 3.7

Think about a situation (e.g. from school, college, work or with friends or family) where you were primarily a follower. Did you come into any of the following categories: Sheep, Yes Person, Alienated Follower, Survivor, Effective Follower, Constructive Dissenter or Destructive Assenter? Maybe you would use another description if not one of these.

In pairs or small groups:

1. Explain what the situation was and the follower role that you adopted, why you adopted it and what your impact on the group was.
2. If you were not an effective follower, what could the leader(s) have done to have enabled you to become one?
3. Share your reflections generally on how important you think followership is to leadership.

Commentary

Hopefully, the activity will have further underlined the importance of followers to leaders and also highlighted the different ways in which leaders and followers relate to each other. Some follower roles are clearly more productive than others. If we think about collective approaches to leadership, leaders need to be able to help followers to be active, to contribute positively and to see themselves as potential leaders in situations when the need arises. It underlines the importance of being group-focused as well as task-focused. For this reason, leaders need to try to understand others' positions, treat people with respect and to be able to communicate what they are trying to achieve. This might also involve having challenging conversations with people who, for one reason or another, are not fully engaged. Another important point is for the leader not to get too preoccupied with maintaining their power and status at the expense of others. Effective leadership is empowering. As Ralph Nader said, the function of leadership is to produce more leaders, not more followers.

Kelley proposes that effective followers can be cultivated in four ways. They are:

1. *Redefining followership and leadership.* Instead of seeing the leadership role as superior to and more active than the role of the follower, we can think of them as equal but different activities.
2. *Honing followership skills.* Training can be offered on subjects such as:
   - improving independent, critical thinking;
   - disagreeing agreeably;

- acting responsibly towards the organisation, the leader, co-workers and oneself;
- similarities and differences between leadership and followership roles;
- moving between the two roles with ease.

3. *Performance evaluation and feedback.* This can be via formal or informal methods.

4. *Organisational structures that encourage followership.* The value of good following needs to be somehow built into the fabric of the organisation.

Much of what Kelley proposes is about the need to make sure that organisational culture and organisational practices both enable and validate effective followership. Everyone needs to feel that they can make a positive contribution to achieving collective goals either by leading, by being a follower who leads or being an effective follower. They are all equally important roles.

To conclude, it is interesting to note that a chapter that started by focusing on definitions of leadership should end stressing the importance of followership and of leader–follower relationships. This suggests that leadership is a much more complex subject than is often supposed and that it cannot solely be understood by focusing on those 'in charge' in organisations. To understand effective leadership requires an understanding, among other things, of how people come together to make sense of the situations that they are in; group dynamics; power differentials in relationships; communication skills; and knowledge of human behaviour and psychology. Fortunately, these are all core areas of knowledge required for social work.

Chapter summary

- Leadership involves making sure the right things get done at the appropriate time, seeing what changes are needed in any given situation and ensuring that they take place.
- Leadership is socially constructed through interaction.
- Leadership is a process whereby an individual influences a group of individuals (followers) to achieve a common goal.
- Leadership and management overlap but are not the same activity. Not all managers are leaders and not all leaders are managers.
- Leadership does not depend on being in a formal position of power. Often people who do not consider themselves as leaders find that they can lead when the situation arises.
- Leadership is about sense-making, relating, visioning and inventing with, perhaps, sense-making being the most important activity.

(Continued)

> (Continued)
>
> - Traditional studies of leadership ignored the relationship between leaders and followers, yet this relationship is one of critical importance.
> - No single model of leadership and no single leader can provide all the answers to the complex problems and challenges facing public services such as social work. Therefore, professional leadership in social work is most appropriately conceptualised as a collective and situational activity where a range of different leadership and (active) followership roles are required from everyone concerned when the situation demands it.

Further reading

Cameron, E and Green, M (2008) *Making sense of leadership*. London: Kogan Page.

This is a thought-provoking book that identifies what are claimed to be five key roles adopted by effective leaders: the Thoughtful Architect; the Tenacious Implementer; the Measured Connector; the Visionary Motivator and the Edgy Catalyser.

Gill, R (2012) *Theory and practice of leadership*. London: Sage.

This book uses examples and case studies to provide a comprehensive review of the major theories of leadership.

Grint, K (2005) *Leadership: Limits and possibilities*. Basingstoke: Palgrave.

This book provides a critical review of the key components of leadership, highlighting the importance of the leader–follower relationship and the importance of followers generally.

Grint, K (2010) *Leadership: A very short introduction*. Oxford: Oxford University Press.

This book provides a very concise and thought-provoking overview of key debates and issues in leadership studies.

MacKian, S and Simons, J (2013) (eds) *Leading, managing, caring*. London: Routledge.

Writing in the context of health and social care, the authors include definitions of leadership, provide a historical perspective of leadership theories and also review leadership theories that influence practice today.

Northouse, P (2015b) *Leadership: Theory and practice* (6th edn). London: Sage.

This is a classic textbook on leadership which provides a clearly written account of major theories and models while using practical exercises that help relate theory to practice.

Roe, K (2017) *Leadership: Practice and perspectives* (2nd edn). Oxford: Oxford University Press.
This is another accessible and practical textbook for those new to leadership studies.

4: Leadership in the Context of Social Work: Limiting and Enabling Factors

Achieving a social work degree

This chapter will enable you to develop the following capabilities to the appropriate level from the PCF:

- knowledge
- critical reflection and analysis
- intervention and skills
- contexts and organisations
- professional leadership
- professionalism.

It will also introduce you to the following academic standards as set out in the social work subject benchmark statement:

5.2   Social Work theory
5.3   Values and ethics
5.4   Service users and carers
5.5   The nature of Social Work practice, in the UK and more widely
5.6   The leadership, organisation and delivery of Social Work services
5.10   Problem-solving skills
5.15   Communication skills
5.16   Skills in working with others
5.17   Skills in personal and professional development

(Continued)

(Continued)

More specifically it will enable you to:

- understand better factors about the wider context in which social work takes place that can either limit or enable the possibilities of professional leadership taking place effectively;
- understand better factors about organisations that can either limit or enable the possibilities of professional leadership taking place effectively;
- appreciate the contribution that professional networks of various kinds can make to professional leadership.

Introduction

In the Introduction to this book it was proposed that 'how you think about leadership will strongly influence how you practise leadership' (Northouse, 2015a, p. 8). In Chapter 3 we discussed how traditional theories of leadership focused on the qualities and activities of 'great men' and that, even today, in many people's eyes, leadership is still regarded primarily as a management responsibility and the province of those at the top of organisations. However, we also discussed how although there are overlaps between the management and leadership, there are also conceptual differences. The point was made that not everyone in a formal management position is a leader, and a leader need not necessarily be someone in a formal management position. We also highlighted that public sector organisations such as the NHS are embracing models that see leadership as a collective and situational activity. These approaches stress that leadership is everyone's responsibility. This view is echoed in professional social work. In Chapter 2 we discussed how, influenced by reports such as that by Eileen Munro (2011), professional leadership is regarded as a capability that needs to be demonstrated by all those involved in social work – from students to senior managers. Professional leadership in social work is now regarded as everyone's responsibility. However, this still leaves us with some rather important questions to answer, not least where and how does professional leadership actually take place? What is supposed to happen? We therefore start the chapter by exploring what professional leadership in the context of social work can mean, making specific reference to how it is described in professional guidance.

We then focus on the various contextual factors that, individually and combined, can have a significant bearing on how and whether effective professional leadership takes place. In this section we discuss the impact of, among other things, financial constraints on public services, bureaucratic and hierarchical organisational structures and managerialism. We then look at other features of organisational cultures that can impact. As part of this discussion we highlight certain aspects of organisational climates such as defensive practices, burnout and groupthink, which can hinder the practice of effective leadership. We conclude the section with a consideration of factors in the physical working environment, such as hot-desking and open plan offices. Such developments highlight what we call the 'paradox of professional leadership', which is when the very working conditions that can make leadership less likely to take place are those that most require effective leadership to change them.

The final section of the chapter focuses on factors that can enable effective professional leadership in social work. These include: the existence of communities of practice, professional networks and organisations that have cultures of learning embedded.

What does professional leadership mean in the context of social work?

In the three previous chapters we have discussed, among other things, ideas about what it means to be a professional, ideas about the role and purpose of social work and also ideas about what leadership involves. All three chapters have demonstrated that each of the concepts under discussion is complex, contested and open to multiple interpretations. To think about professional leadership in the context of social work involves thinking about how these three problematic concepts fit together. It would therefore be reasonable to assume that what professional leadership in social work involves is also contestable and open to different interpretations. How we approach this will depend on what we understand social work to be, what we take 'professional' to mean and then, obviously, what we believe leadership involves. Therefore, to talk of professional leadership might suggest, to some, the process of helping to create a new vision for social work to meet the many challenges of the twenty-first century, working out what direction social work should be going in and then thinking about how to get it there. To others, professional leadership might be more a question of focusing on the functions that social work currently fulfils in society and working to improve standards of professionalism so that the current system works better. As discussed in Chapters 1 and 2, much rests on what we think constitutes professionalism. To some, this might mean making social work into more of a profession in terms of developing its expertise and authority, but also its status and power. For others, this might mean making social work as open and democratic as possible in order to minimise power differences and make it more of an inclusive activity. The brief history of social work that was included in Chapter 2 illustrated that there is never just one path along which social work can be led. Not only are the various contexts in which social work takes place always changing, social work itself is also always in a state of flux as it tries to respond to the many demands made upon it.

Therefore, anyone involved in professional leadership in social work, in whatever capacity, needs to understand the various contexts in which social work takes place. This will include changing global, national and local contexts; changes in the economy; changes in society;

changes in politics; and changes in legislation and policy. All of which, of course, are often interlinked. That is not to say that you have to be an expert in any of these areas, but you need to have a sense of what factors are driving the current social work agenda. If you have no sense of this then your role can only be that of a follower reliant on others' versions of what is happening and what should be done.

As we discussed in the previous chapter, 'sense-making' is an important role of leadership – part of this being to ask the questions 'what are we supposed to be doing?' and 'why?' at the appropriate time and to the appropriate people. But then, as we also saw, an important part of leading is also contributing to answering these questions to the best of our ability. And, again, this will not be coming up with all the answers single-handedly, but taking part in collective discussions both within the profession and with other stakeholders. In this respect, a fundamental task of leadership is to be active rather than passive in making sure that you ask the right questions and that you are sufficiently informed. As we will discuss further in Chapter 5, both research-mindedness and critical reflection are important leadership skills.

If we are going to contribute to professional leadership we cannot expect to simply perform the role of social worker passively and unthinkingly. We need to be prepared to understand the bigger picture, use our initiative, ask questions, exchange ideas with others and develop our own thinking about what good social work is. However, that cannot be done without reference to existing professional frameworks. We cannot simply invent our own idea of social work. There need to be collectively agreed aims and objectives to mandate what is done. In this respect it is important to understand fully what is contained in current regulatory and professional guidance about the roles, tasks and capabilities required in social work. Therefore, in the following section we turn our attention to what guidance tells us about what is expected in terms of professional leadership.

Professional leadership in the professional guidance in social work

The *Professional Capabilities Framework* (PCF) was introduced in 2012 as the overarching framework of guidance for professional standards in social work in England. It comprises nine levels that encompass everyone involved in professional social work, from those at entry level through to those working at strategic levels of senior management. It consists of nine domains of capabilities. For the first time in any professional social work guidance, professional leadership was included as a required capability. Subsequently, various 'Knowledge and skills statements' have been produced, aimed at specific areas of social work (see Chapter 2) and they have been mapped onto the PCF. When the PCF was refreshed in 2017/2018 (BASW, 2017) some key changes were made in how professional leadership was described. The statement from BASW (2018b) below explains both the changes and the rationale behind them.

PROFESSIONAL LEADERSHIP – Promote the profession and good social work practice. Take responsibility for the professional learning and development of others. Develop personal influence and be part of the collective leadership and impact of the profession.

Original

The social work profession evolves through the contribution of its members in activities such as practice research, supervision, assessment of practice, teaching and management. An individual's contribution will gain influence when undertaken as part of a learning, practice-focused organisation. Learning may be facilitated with a wide range of people including social work colleagues, service users and carers, volunteers, foster carers and other professionals.

New

We act and show leadership, individually and collectively, through promoting social work's purpose, practices and impact. We achieve this through activities such as: advancing practice; supervising; educating others; research; evaluation; using innovation and creativity; writing; presenting; using social media; being active in professional networks and bodies; influencing; challenging; contributing to policy; taking formal leadership/management roles. We promote organisational contexts conducive to good practice and learning. We work in partnership with people who use services and stakeholders in developing our leadership and aims for the profession.

Rationale for change

This domain was particularly covered in the review of the PCF in 2015, commissioned by the College of Social Work. The consultation in 2017 substantiated the need for change. The focus of this domain descriptor has been changed to emphasise the importance and potential impact of both individual and collective engagement in 'leadership activities'. Key examples of these are expanded from the short list in the original version.

The title descriptor has not been changed as it was stronger than the text below it. The text below now more effectively expands on the title descriptor.

The importance of developing the profession, and how we shape our leadership actions, in conjunction with people who use services and other stakeholders is emphasised.

The importance of using professional leadership to influence the context in which social work operates is emphasised.

https://www.basw.co.uk/pcf/

The way that professional leadership is defined and explained in the PCF indicates that it is based on a collective model of leadership. In the original descriptor professional leadership is defined in terms of a relatively narrow range of activities with a lot of emphasis placed on leading through teaching, learning and through the development of self and others. The revised descriptor conceptualises professional leadership as a much wider and diverse set of activities, capturing many of the broader leadership roles and activities discussed in Chapter 3, such as 'using innovation and creativity' and 'influencing, challenging and contributing to policy'. It is encouraging to see 'the importance of using professional leadership to influence the context in which social work operates is emphasised' included in the rationale for change, as many would argue that social work has a leadership role to play in various types of social and political campaigning (McKitterick, 2015). Perhaps this aspect of leadership could have been mentioned even more explicitly, linking it to other domains such as 'Rights and Justice' and 'Contexts and Organisations', for example.

The rationale provided could have also acknowledged more explicitly that professional social work is not a 'settled' discipline or occupation. Social work has always been a contested activity that both takes place within and reflects a set of interrelated, ever changing contexts. In the previous chapter we talked about the importance of 'sense-making' (Ancona et al., 2007) as a core leadership capability. This could have been highlighted both in the original and revised version of the PCF. Arguably, before we can innovate and influence we need to be able to 'make sense' of the complexities of what is going on in society and also what social work's role and purpose is within it. However, overall, the shift in how professional leadership is interpreted in the PCF is to be welcomed, although how it is interpreted and put into practice remains to be seen at the time of writing.

Lastly, while the level descriptors (BASW, 2018b) make it clear that professional leadership is the responsibility of everyone either in professional practice or training to be in the profession, it is quite possible that some readers might still need convincing that any form of leadership is beyond them because of their junior position or because they are inexperienced or unqualified. However, let it be reiterated, the professional leadership domain is on a par with the others; it is not a special domain that requires qualities only possessed by a few. The more that you think about (and make sense of) what professional social work is and engage in conversations with others, the more opportunities for leadership will emerge. In Chapter 5, we discuss in more detail how professional leadership can be put into practice. This will include taking a closer look at sense-making. However, next we return to look at contextual factors that either enable or hinder professional leadership opportunities in social work.

Professional leadership: Limiting factors

As we have discussed, social work takes place in a variety of contexts: social, economic, policy, organisational and so on. In this section we examine selected important contextual factors that can limit or constrain the possibilities for leadership in social work, either on their own or often in combination with each other. In the following section we will examine how some of these effects can be countered.

Economic and financial factors

For some years, adults' and children's social work in England has been taking place in a context of rising demand and with less money being spent on it in real terms. For example, real public spending on social care organised by English local authorities fell by 1.0 per cent between 2009–10 and 2015–16. Within this, spending on adult social care fell by 6.4 per cent, during a period when the population aged 65 and above grew by 15.6 per cent (IFS, 2017). With children's services, spending has fallen by 9 per cent since 2010, with the numbers of children in need rising by 5 per cent (Guardian, 2017a). Working under financial pressures does not, in itself, limit leadership. In fact, arguably, when such pressures bear down on social work, professional leadership is all the more important, especially around prioritising effort and trying to maintain social work values. However, as the case study below will illustrate, there are significant knock-on effects when social workers work in the context of deep and prolonged cuts in public spending. We will use the case study to examine the potential limiting effects on professional leadership.

Case study 4.1   Social workers working through illness to keep up with caseloads

Social workers are working through illness or putting in extra unpaid hours just to keep up with their caseloads, a study has found. The survey of more than 1,200 social workers found 60% said they had worked when they should have taken time off sick on at least two occasions over the past year.

Researchers also found social workers worked an average of 10 extra hours each week, which equated to £600m unpaid overtime per year when applied to the entire UK social work workforce. Bath Spa University carried out the study, with support from the British Association of Social Workers and the Social Workers Union.

Jermaine Ravalier, the study's lead author, said the results showed the satisfaction social workers got from their jobs 'can no longer outweigh the lack of support they are experiencing'. He said: 'Deep budget cuts are forcing social workers to take on more cases than ever, putting them under pressure to deliver a service to people that are often vulnerable with fewer resources. In order to keep up, they are simply giving away days of their personal time.

'If this keeps up, and the social workers we spoke with do leave the profession, local authorities will be forced to pay for contract workers who are expensive, transient and certainly won't be working lots of free hours.'

$\longrightarrow$

> *The research found social workers were 'moderately to highly engaged' in their jobs, but were put under 'significant strain' by organisational factors, such as poor working conditions. Forty per cent of respondents said they were dissatisfied with their jobs and half wanted to quit within the next year-and-a-half. These feelings were stronger among children's social workers than adults' or independent social workers. Asked about what would improve working conditions, social workers said they wanted to see reduced caseloads, better managerial support and supervision, and steps taken to address the 'blame culture' affecting the profession.*
>
> Extracts taken from *Community Care, 2017c*

Social work in a context of budget cuts, rising workloads and 'blame culture'

There are various interrelated issues raised in the case study. Due to budget cuts in both adults' and children's services, social workers' working conditions are deteriorating, caseloads are increasing, some workers are putting in extra hours unpaid and stress levels are rising to the point where a significant number of social workers are taking time off work due to ill health. Those social workers surveyed said that they wanted better managerial support and supervision, and steps taken to address the 'blame culture'.

These particular budget cuts need to be understood in the context of a programme of austerity that successive governments have been implementing in the UK since the financial crisis of 2007–8. However, there is a broader historical, economic and political context to understand. Since the mid-1980s, strongly influenced by neoliberalism (Crouch, 2011), successive Conservative and New Labour governments have tried to shrink the public sector and have opted for small, year-to-year reductions in the growth of overall public spending (Hood and Himaz, undated). In times when social deprivation and associated problems are increasing (Backwith, 2015) and the number of people living into deep old age is also increasing, it can be expected that this will result in more referrals to social workers. If, at the same time, resources are being cut, then this will explain the increased pressures felt by those working in the personal social services.

Studies have shown that there are links between budget cuts, increased caseloads, work pressures, high staff turnover and social worker 'burnout' (see, for example, McFadden, 2015). The staff shortages resulting from these factors have increased the reliance on agency workers to plug gaps. This has led to much social work being delivered by a transient workforce (Bowyer and Rowe, 2015). Capacity for professional leadership can be impaired under such conditions because many workers' primary focus inevitably becomes self-protection rather than concern about others or the profession generally. In circumstances where there is constant pressure our orientation to work can easily become reactive rather than proactive.

Practice becomes 'dead' and 'automated' rather than 'inspiring' and 'engaged' (Ferguson, 2014); a factor that might impact on social workers' willingness as well as their capacity to demonstrate professional leadership might be the presence of a 'blame culture'. The article does not elaborate this point but, where such cultures exist in organisations and in society generally, this would incline many workers to keep their heads down rather than speak up and possibly attract more blame. An equally worrying effect of working in a culture of blame or fear is the development of defensive practices (Whittaker and Harvard, 2016). Satyamurti (1981) found that, when under pressure and feeling under threat from outside, social workers can seek solidarity among themselves by developing a siege mentality, part of which is to negatively stereotype outsiders. This can include the media, management, other professionals and even service users.

The state of affairs described in the case study evidently requires some form of professional leadership for various reasons. These include: to protect the service, to safeguard service users, to protect the workforce and to promote social work values. However, we have discussed how such conditions are not propitious for social workers to take the initiative and assume leadership roles. This is certainly true as far as individual social workers and junior managers are concerned. However, this is where it is important to work collectively. Greater strength and influence can be derived from the solidarity that comes from collective activity. It is also important for those away from the frontline to recognise the challenges faced by ordinary frontline social workers and to step in accordingly. There is leadership in evidence in this article. It comes from Bath Spa University, BASW and SWU working together, gathering evidence and using it to bring the issues into the public domain. This highlights how important it is for individuals, either as leaders or followers, to work collaboratively and to network, as we shall discuss more in the next chapter. However, acknowledgement also needs to be given to *Community Care* magazine, which relaunched its Stand up for Social Work campaign to raise the profile of social work in what was an election year (i.e. 2015) precisely to gain recognition for social work at a time of budget cuts and increased demand. However, we discussed in Chapter 3 how effective leadership involves influencing others and producing change. Therefore, apart from bringing the issues into the public domain, we need to think about how and whether the actions taken by *Community Care*, Bath Spa University, BASW and SWU have improved matters. Simply stating the problem, however passionately and however well-evidenced, does not necessarily mean that leadership will be effective in producing change. There have to be some realistic suggestions as to what needs to be done. Perhaps more importantly, it also requires a receptive audience among policy-makers and other political decision-makers.

In summary, the case study illustrates how economic and financial factors can both limit the potential for professional leadership in social work and also create the need for such leadership at the same time (see the section on the 'paradox of professional leadership' later in this section). It underlines how, when the economic, financial and political context is unfavourable, leadership can only be effective if people work together collectively and involve themselves in concerted political action rather than try to do things separately or on an individual basis. It is interesting to note that, a month after the article was published, the trade union UNISON announced that not only they but also a variety of the UK's main social work organisations, including BASW, SWAN, the Joint University Council Social Work Education Committee, the Association of Professors of Social Work and other relevant trade unions, the University and College Union and the Social Workers Union had agreed to campaign collectively to safeguard social work (UNISON, 2015). At the time of writing, some three years later, it is still hard to say how effective the campaign was in achieving its aims. Many of the core problems persist. However, arguably, some progress is better than no progress at all. The voices speaking up for social work were all the stronger for being united. As was highlighted above, professional leadership in social work is limited in how far it can protect the profession's interests if the political and economic climate is unfavourable.

Managerialism and hierarchical bureaucratic organisations

The article talked about the negatives on social worker morale of a 'blame culture'. This was probably alluding to attitudes prevalent in certain sections of the media and society generally, which hold negative ideas about the work that social workers do and the way that they do it. In this culture, regardless of what other factors might be responsible in the wider system and how complex the issues might be, individual practitioners tend to be blamed and scapegoated when anything goes wrong. Social work leaders have generally found it difficult to push back against such attitudes for a variety of reasons (Barrow, 2017).

Blame cultures can also exist *within* social work organisations. This usually means that individual practitioners are blamed when things go wrong rather than seeing the problem as either one of system or organisational failure or failure of management (Ayers, 2017). This brings the topic of organisational cultures into sharper focus. Later, we will discuss how organisational cultures can enable professional leadership, but, first, in this section, we concentrate on organisational cultures that obstruct or limit the potential for professional leadership. Specifically, we are going to look at the impact of working in bureaucratic and hierarchical organisations, as well as that of managerialism on organisations.

Although grouped together for the purposes of this discussion, hierarchical bureaucracies and managerialism should not be regarded as the same thing. However, because most professional social work takes place in bureaucratic organisations and these organisations have been subjected to managerialisation in recent decades (Clarke and Newman, 1997; Harris and White, 2009), the two organisational processes combined have helped to create the conditions in which most contemporary social work takes place (Howe, 2014). We will take each element in turn, starting with bureaucracies.

Bureaucratic hierarchical organisations

Bureaucracies have acquired a bad name – or at least the term 'bureaucratic' has. We have come to associate anything bureaucratic with endless 'red tape' and unnecessary procedures. The negative stereotype of a bureaucracy is of an organisation suffering from some form of institutional sclerosis. That is to say that it is so rule-bound and rigid in its working practices that it is unable to respond quickly, if at all, to any demands made upon it. It works for itself rather than its service users. However, despite this popular stereotype, both in theory and in practice, compared to other forms of organisation, bureaucracies are considered as the most rational, efficient and fair way to administer public services (du Gay, 2000). However, in order to operate in these ways, bureaucracies need to be run on clearly defined rules and procedures. So, if someone applies or is referred for a service, their application should be processed against the same eligibility criteria and in the same way as all other such claims. No one should be able to receive favourable treatment, nor should anyone be discriminated against for whatever reason. However, in reality, every referral or application seldom gets exactly the same attention. Because of the complexity and variety of decision-making that is required in bureaucratic organisations, together with the fact that demand for services always outstrips supply, some interpretation of the rules and therefore use of discretion by the people that work in the organisation is unavoidable. Without this the organisation could not function. This is where potential favouritism and prejudicial behaviour can creep in, either intentionally or unintentionally (Lipsky, 1980). Supervision of the workforce is therefore required by managers to ensure that rules and procedures are followed properly. However, because managers operate in the same environment, they too are required to exercise discretion in how the rules are put into practice (Evans, 2010). Therefore, while the theory of bureaucratic organisation is based on the impartial application of rules and procedures, it is in the nature of bureaucracies in real life that, at all points of the organisational hierarchy, practitioners and managers are able to use a degree of discretion in how the work is done. In fact, if this was not possible, bureaucracies would almost certainly grind to a halt.

We discussed in Chapters 1 and 2 that it is considered to be the mark of professionals that, because of the nature and complexity of the decisions they are required to make, they require professional expertise. In such situations we therefore accept that professionals should have the autonomy to use their professional judgement in decision-making. We also discussed in earlier chapters that social workers are required to make professional decisions, but within a bureaucratic organisational environment. That is to say, their professional autonomy is constrained by rules and procedures over which the managerial hierarchy, not they, have control. Hence, it was explained that writers such as Clarke and Newman (1997) described social work as a 'bureau-profession' because it combines elements of professionalism with a bureaucratic framework.

Since personal social services departments were first introduced, there have never been enough resources to meet demand (Glasby, 2005). Managers have always had to decide how to prioritise services and ensure that their organisations work within statutory guidelines. Social workers have always had to comply with the rules and procedures laid down in policy and interpreted by their organisations. Even though most social services managers were also qualified social workers, from time to time there would be disagreements about what the 'professional' thing to do was in certain cases. Such decisions were usually informed by various factors, including: interpretation of the legislation, reference to organisational guidance and a professional discussion based on social work knowledge and values. Ultimately, despite enjoying considerable discretion in what they did, practitioners could not make important decisions without managerial approval. Therefore, social work has never been carried out by social workers acting as autonomous professionals. However, in the decades immediately after Seebohm, managers were generally prepared to trust their social workers to practise with only a light managerial touch – especially the more experienced practitioners. In broad terms, while there were obviously variations from one office to another, the overall climate in social work was that, for better or for worse, social workers were trusted to act like professionals with the minimum of managerial oversight.

In Chapter 2 we looked at the impact of managerialism on public services and social work in particular. Managerialism, in the abstract, is the imposition of performance management methods in order, among other things, to increase productivity and make public services more business-like. Harris and White (2009) referred to this as focusing on the three 'E's' – Economy, Efficiency and Effectiveness. Compared as ideal types, managerialist organisational culture is dramatically at odds with professional organisational culture. For example, managerialism is largely about targets, procedures, ticking boxes and productivity, while professionalism is about working autonomously, making professional judgements according to professional expertise and professional ethics and values. In black and white terms, in one system management has total power over work practices and in the other the professional is autonomous in practice. In social work a simplistic view would regard the supplanting of professionalism by managerialism as a *fait accompli*. However, as was highlighted in Chapter 2, the actual reality in social work is less distinct. As writers such as Kirkpatrick (2006) and White and Harris (2007) have argued, while managerialism has definitely taken a grip on social work organisations since the 1980s, this has not been in a uniform way, nor in a way that has squeezed out all possibility of professional discretion in how social work is practised (Evans, 2010). As we also saw the Munro report (2011) has positively argued for the return of professional judgement into social work practice. So, we need to avoid taking too simplistic a view about how managerialism has transformed social work. However, be that as it may, most social work organisations do bear the hallmarks of managerialisation in some shape or form. Some writers are scathing about the effects of managerialism on professional social work. For example, Rogowski (2011, p. 157), writing about social work with children and families has claimed: 'Practitioners' success is now often simply measured in terms of whether managers' targets have been met. The result is that scope for a progressive, even radical/critical, practice is greatly reduced, though spaces that remain need to be utilised'.

Rogowski's opinion is not untypical and has also been applied to other branches of social work (Lymbery and Postle, 2007; Harris and White, 2009). Despite efforts to reprofessionalise social work in recent years (Munro, 2011; Goodman and Trowler, 2012) it would be fair to say that, combined with the squeeze on resources discussed earlier, the managerialisation of social work has curtailed professional autonomy and constrained professional leadership.

Activity 4.1   The challenges presented by managerialism to professional leadership in social work

Taking the quotation from Rogowski above as a starting point, return to Chapter 2 and familiarise yourself with what the managerialisation of social work entails and the various ways it can impact on practice.

Questions

1. In what ways might managerialism limit the potential for professional leadership?
2. Why does the managerialisation of social work make professional leadership all the more important?

Commentary

There are various ways in which managerialism can limit professional leadership in social work. By shifting power to managers, whose own performance is predominately assessed against quantitative criteria, social work organisations have tended to focus on 'throughput' and meeting performance targets. Also, the increased use of IT in social work organisations has contributed towards greater proceduralisation of social work practice, at the same time making it more visible to managerial inspection (MacDonald, 2006). Coupled with cuts in resources and the pressures discussed in the previous section, this has led to an intensification of the work process (Harris and White, 2009). Therefore, not only has managerialisation increased managerial oversight, curtailing practitioners' use of professional discretion to some degree, the increasingly intensified and more pressurised work experience means that the space and opportunities for practitioners to reflect critically upon their practice and to focus on qualitative aspects such as relationships and feelings are restricted (Knott and Scragg, 2016). Diaz and Drewery (2016) have also highlighted the negative impact of managerialism on evidence-based practice. They argue that:

> *When busy social workers have large caseloads, it is understandable that they do not have the opportunity to be aware of what the evidence suggests works. Their main priority and that of their manager is ensuring that targets are met and that those service users most at risk are safeguarded, there is simply not the time to practice* [sic] *in an evidence based manner.*

Ibid., p. 428

Therefore, while it is not the only factor, managerialism has significantly contributed towards social work becoming both a more proceduralised and more intensified occupation in recent decades. This has limited time and space for both critical reflection and research to inform practice (Gould and Baldwin, 2004).

Given the various issues facing professional social work highlighted above and in previous sections, the risk is that professional judgement, professional decision-making and professional social work practice generally will become greatly impaired by factors such as lack of time, lack of resources and an impoverished professional culture in social work organisations. This is why professional leadership, although difficult in such circumstances, is all the more important. The fundamental quality of the service is at stake. This means that some of society's most vulnerable groups will be negatively affected. As most social work service users have little or no power that they can exercise to advocate for themselves, a lack of professional leadership means that not only are social workers working in very challenging circumstances, but also service users' lives are placed at risk in different ways. One would hope that social work managers working at the strategic level in organisations would tackle this, but organisational pressures are often so strong and loyalties often so divided that strategic professional leadership in organisations can become compromised and diluted. In such situations it requires the collective efforts of the whole profession to take action to effect change.

In this section we have identified several important contextual factors that potentially limit the possibility of effective professional leadership in social work but, at the same time, underline its importance. We have discussed how working in bureaucratic and managerialised organisations can encourage styles of social work that are process driven and dominated by the need to meet quantitative targets. Under those conditions, professional standards of social work practice can become eroded as the work becomes a routinised form of people processing. The space for critical reflection and professional dialogue becomes squeezed out. This presents such an important challenge for professional leadership that it requires everyone in professional social work to take responsibility and play a part.

The impact of organisational cultures and climate

We have discussed how social work practice takes place in organisations that are affected by the broader political and economic climate, the processes of managerialisation and other 'macro' factors (UNISON, 2016). However, each social work organisation also has its own specific organisational culture or micro 'climate' which is influenced by macro factors but also by organisation-specific factors (Holt and Lawler, 2005). In this section, we focus on the implications for professional leadership of certain ways of working and thinking, team cultures, emotional contexts, behaviours and mindsets that can develop in social work organisations for different reasons. Again, these need to be understood in their wider context. We have already touched on some of them such as burnout, stress, defensive practices and low motivation, all of which deplete mental energy and diminish both interest in and enthusiasm for the job of social work. There are, however, other aspects of work cultures in organisations that can limit the potential for effective professional leadership.

Defensive practices, logical fallacies and other problematic behaviours in organisations

To be effective, professional leadership requires both leaders and followers to be actively working together in constructive relationships. It also requires, among other things, that everyone involved is open to constructive criticism, is prepared to engage in creative problem-solving and is able to embrace new ideas and ways of working. However, within organisations individuals or, more often, groups of individuals can get stuck in certain patterns of thinking and behaving. We will explore some of these below. However, first a case study will serve to illustrate some of the mindsets and behaviours in question.

Case study 4.2   Community Outreach

Valerie is manager of an adult social care team in a rural area. Budgets are tight and demand for services, particularly among the older population, is rising. At a meeting of managers in her county it was decided that Valerie's team would trial a new 'preventive' outreach strategy designed to divert lower-level cases to the voluntary sector and other services in the community so that the team could concentrate more on the more complex cases involving higher levels of risk and need. The scheme requires social workers from the team to attend a different village community centre three times per week to

→

enable the public to attend drop-in sessions. This will be alongside representatives from health-services, a Citizens Advice financial advisor and selected local voluntary organisations. The idea is that people or their carers can drop in and discuss their problems and if they meet the criteria for a social care service then a referral will be taken. However, the emphasis is on exploring alternatives to statutory services using existing resources in the community. Advice will also be given on how to stay healthy longer and to promote well-being generally.

When Valerie explains the proposal at a team meeting, it is met with a general lack of enthusiasm. Most of the team have worked together for several years. As a team they opposed the proposal. Common comments were:

'This won't work, we tried something like this in the 1990s and it just turned out to be a complete waste of time.'

'With my caseload, I just wouldn't have the space. I can't sit and twiddle my thumbs in a dusty church hall three times a week, talking to some bod from Citizens Advice.'

'If management are so keen on this, why doesn't one of them do it?'

'This won't cut down the safeguarding referrals. Someone who is being abused isn't going to just turn up at a community centre.'

'That's a good point, how do we know we're going to be safe there? Anyone can come in.'

'I see one of the days is supposed to be Wednesday. That won't work; it's panel that day.'

'Why can't we just leave leaflets there? If people want to speak to us the number's on the leaflet or they could email us.'

'This sounds like another one of Greg Grainger's (the service manager) bright ideas designed to curry favour with the Councillors, while adding to our workload.'

At the end of the meeting, Irene, one of the longer-serving members, turns to Valerie and says: 'Look, you can see that it's not that we haven't given it some thought, but the team is pretty much 100 per cent against it. It's not going to help us do our job better. In fact, to my mind, it will make it worse. Maybe you can feed that back to the senior management? We're better off staying as we are.'

Two newer members of the team had remained silent. The problem for Valerie and the other managers was that the existing system was not working either. There was known to be a lot of lower-level need that was not being met and situations were being allowed to deteriorate.

Questions

1. What are your reactions to the team's responses in this scenario?
2. What are the implications in terms of professional leadership?

Commentary

The team's negative response to the proposal might have been justified, but much of the 'argument' or 'evidence' given to support the decision seemed to be rather subjective, *ad hoc* and indicative of a general disposition against adopting new ideas. It appears from the comments as if many of the team had prejudged the issue. It seems they were happy to maintain their normal working patterns despite the fact that the system was under strain and not working that well for the public. There might even have been an element of the 'siege mentality' referred to earlier. The decision was presented as one that belonged to the whole team, even though two members had not communicated their views. This was possibly because they were relatively new to the team and anxious about not fitting in with the prevailing attitudes.

The team climate could be said to reflect a certain cynicism or jadedness towards the job. Again, this might well be justified in certain situations. However, teams where cynicism and jadedness become entrenched are harder to lead because they are likely to have become stuck in certain ways of thinking and working that preclude the possibility of things changing for the better – whatever is being suggested. Therefore, the team could be said to be stuck because, even though the current state of affairs is evidently not working that satisfactorily, they are not particularly receptive to new ideas and are seemingly content to keep working the way they are.

Many of the team seem to have the characteristics of 'Alienated Followers' that were described in Chapter 3. However, there is something more. Irene has taken on a leadership role herself. She appears not only to be talking for the group, she also seems to be presenting an alternative vision in terms of what would and would not enable the team to do their job better. Arguably, she has mobilised the Alienated Followers in the team better than Valerie in this respect, albeit in a way that resists change and maintains the status quo. Lurking behind the two positions is a very interesting and important question: what is the most professional way forward in terms of social work? The case study shows that it cannot be assumed that effective professional leadership will necessarily come from management decisions or from experienced practitioners taking the lead. It also illustrates that not only is it possible to hold different ideas about how to 'do' social work in any given situation, but also that such ideas are not always explicitly informed by what is most in service users' interests or consideration of the core tasks of social work. In the scenario, no one argued their case with reference to professional social work values.

Demotivated mindsets, limiting beliefs, logical fallacies and groupthink

The case study drew our attention to the fact that social work teams and subgroups within teams can develop ways of thinking and working that are demotivated, defensive and both wary about and resistant to change. This should not simply be dismissed as sheer bloody-mindedness. This type of development needs to be understood in its wider context. Teams can become defensive in their outlook for a variety of reasons. It can be because of the increased intensity and stressfulness of work due to the sheer volume of referrals ('bombardment' rates) and the need to hit organisational performance targets (McKitterick, 2015). However, defensiveness also arises because of the stressful nature of the work itself, as we will discuss later in this section. Often it is a combination of both (Coffey, Dugdill and Tattersall, 2004; UNISON, 2016).

Teams (or individuals within teams) can also become apathetic in response to new ideas because they have tried to instigate, influence or resist organisational developments in the past, but with no success. They have not been listened to. As a consequence, they develop limiting beliefs about their own efficacy and effectiveness in what they are able to achieve. Hardcastle (2011) sees this as form of 'learned helplessness' (Seligman, 1972) – a negative state of mind that comes from the repeated failure to exert influence over decisions that affect one's working life. Such negative attitudes are more likely to be evident in organisations which have a culture of 'macho management' or where there is a history of bullying by managers. Again, it is important to be aware of the specific organisational context when exploring why there might be limitations to professional leadership.

Notwithstanding the reasons, the kinds of responses seen in the case study are not uncommon. Therefore, it is useful to be aware of the kinds of 'stuck' behaviours and defensive mindsets that can develop, together with different strategies that are adopted to resist the consideration of new initiatives and the possibility of change. The more that we are aware of the potential pitfalls of getting into negative habits of mind, the less likely it is that we will allow ourselves (and others) to fall into them. If we can recognise and guard against this, the better the chances of practising more effectively and with a greater feeling of professional satisfaction. This all creates a more positive environment for professional leadership.

Logical fallacies

According to Hardcastle (2011, p. 187), a logical fallacy is: 'a misconception based on deceptive or false appearance and deceitfulness, or fraud'. This definition might sound rather judgemental, as if people who adopt logical fallacies always deliberately set out to deceive or defraud others. However, often people fall into employing such fallacies without too much deliberation or conscious thought. Hardcastle argues that logical fallacies are commonly used to either promote or (as in the case presented in Case study 4.2) oppose change. He cites Gambrill and Gibbs (2009), who listed nine common logical fallacies:

1. Ad hominem *(at the person): Attacking (or praising) the person, or feeling attacked (or praised) as a person, rather than examining and staying on the substance of an argument regardless of its presenter. It personalizes the position.*

2. *Appeal to authority* (ad verecundium*): An attempt to bully an opponent into accepting a conclusion by attributing the conclusion, truthfully or not, to a higher authority or recognized expert and playing on the opponent's reluctance to question the conclusion of someone who has a high status or is viewed as the expert.*

3. *Diversion (red herring): An attempt to sidetrack people from one argument by introducing another argument, usually more inflammatory, so as to never deal effectively with the first position.*

4. *Stereotyping: Oversimplifying about a class of arguments or the people making them by using negative labelling, profiling and social identities.*

5. *Manner or style: Believing or rejecting an argument because of the apparent sincerity, speaking voice, attractiveness, stage presence, likability, or other stylistic traits of an argument's presenter.*

6. *Groupthink: The tendency for group members (for example, of interdisciplinary teams, task groups, service-coordination groups, staff) to avoid sharing useful opinions or data with the group because they fear they might be criticized, might hurt the feelings of other group members, or might cause disunity.*

7. *Bandwagon: This fallacy relies on the phrases 'they say' (usually an unknown they) and 'everyone is doing it or knows it' (usually an unspecified everyone) – so you had better get on the bandwagon.*

8. *Either/or (false dilemma): Stating or implying that there are only two alternative positions available and one, the opposing position, is usually untenable. This fallacy denies the opportunity to explore the true range of options.*

9. *Straw man argument: Misrepresenting a person's argument and then attacking the misrepresentation as obviously a bad choice (Gambrill and Gibbs, 2009, pp. 116–19).*

Adapted from Hardcastle (2011, p. 187)

Certain of the fallacies listed seemed to be evident in the Community Outreach discussion. It would be surprising if you had not encountered them (or even used them!) yourself at various times. Such ways of thinking and talking can come very easily at times. However, the important point is that, left unchallenged in oneself and others, they present blocks both to critical reflection generally and, more specifically, to effective professional leadership.

We need to be mindful of different logical fallacies, particularly those that draw in and impact negatively on others. Because much of decision-making in social work is collective, we now focus attention on the phenomenon of 'groupthink'. It is a useful concept to understand because, if it is not identified and checked, not only can it limit professional leadership, it can also be responsible for seriously flawed decisions being made.

Groupthink

The concept of groupthink was developed by the American psychologist Irving Janis. While it was not developed from studying social work, it is not difficult to see how it might apply in many social work situations. Janis (1982, p. 12) defined groupthink as:

> *a mode of thinking people engage in when they are deeply involved in a cohesive in-group, when the members' striving for unanimity override their motivation to realistically appraise alternative courses of action. Groupthink refers to a deterioration of mental efficiency, reality testing, and moral judgment that results from in-group pressures.*

Groupthink therefore occurs when a group of people who work closely together have a tendency to make decisions without sufficiently challenging each other and without analysing and evaluating their ideas critically. Conflict is minimised to preserve group harmony and cohesion. People confirm each other's bias. Groupthink is more likely to occur when groups work together very closely and when they are under considerable pressure to make important decisions. Because of a desire to preserve group cohesion, coupled with an unwillingness to stick out from the group, individual members are reluctant to challenge decisions. This feeds into uncritical and irrational thinking. As a consequence, decisions made under the influence of groupthink have a low probability of achieving successful outcomes. Groupthink is more likely to develop when there are vague terms of reference; flawed organisational processes and procedures; when strong subgroups are allowed to become insulated from wider networks; and also because of poor leadership.

If you think back to the scenario in the case study, some of the team's responses could be seen as examples of groupthink, as well as other logical fallacies.

Organisational defensive practices in response to anxiety

We have highlighted that in social work organisations the specific organisational climate can be influenced by a range of factors including: pressures arising from negative media attention; rising demand and budget cuts; the bombardment rate of referrals; and managerial practices. We have indicated that this can create the conditions for both negative mindsets and depleted mental energy among those who work in such organisations. This can clearly pose obstacles for professional leadership. However, defensive practices can also develop from the nature of the work itself. In social work, sometimes the degree of risk is so great, the stories of the service users so horrendous and the stakes so high in relation to decision-making that levels of anxiety lead to various forms of defensive practice. Drawing on the work of Menzies (1960) in the field of hospital nursing, Taylor, Becket and McKeigue (2007) examined how social workers in child protection and childcare teams coped with working with high levels of anxiety. They identified a range of defensive practices that closely echoed Menzies' earlier work. They were all strategies that were a response to high levels of anxiety. They included: projection, ritual task performance, checking and splitting.

Projection

In Menzies' original study (1960) nurses dealt with their anxieties by 'projecting' responsibility upwards to their superiors. In the study by Taylor et al. the social workers were as likely to project their anxieties across this wider system, such as other professionals, as up the organisational hierarchy.

Ritual task performance

Menzies observed that, rather than use their initiative or discretion, nurses dealt with emotionally charged life-or-death work by engaging in ritual task performance – following procedures rigidly. This had the effect of depersonalising individual patients and helping the nurses to control difficult feelings. As Taylor et al. (2007, p. 29) comment, 'procedures bring a sense of security in the face of anxiety and doubt'. They found that social workers also dealt with anxiety by following procedures in a way that depersonalised service users. It had echoes of what Lipsky (1980) described as a 'people processing' mentality, when feeling the threat of being overwhelmed emotionally.

Checking and rechecking

Menzies found that nurses in the hospital diluted the sense of responsibility for difficult decision-making by making continual checks and counter-checks. This was not only found to be a way of spreading responsibility as widely as possible, it was also a way of postponing difficult action as long as possible. Taylor et al. (2007) identified similar processes going on with social workers. This type of behaviour provides the illusion of purposeful activity, but one of its important purposes is to insulate practitioners from bearing the responsibility for taking emotionally difficult decisions.

Splitting

Menzies (1960, p. 101) observed that 'the core of the anxiety situation for the nurse lies in her relation with the patient'. Therefore, the anxiety became easier to cope with if split into manageable parts. From the social work study, Taylor et al. (2007, p. 30) also observed splitting behaviours, concluding:

> *Social work organizations are shaped by the anxieties of the wider society as well as those of the workers in immediate contact with service users, and for both the tendency is to deal with these anxieties by splitting them into more apparently manageable tasks. But what is lost is an awareness of the complexity of the whole, and the anxiety remains while the limits of knowledge and control are not faced.*

Summary

This section has discussed some of the key factors about organisations that can combine to create mindsets and behaviours among practitioners and managers that could be described variously as demotivated, defensive, uncritical, negative, jaded and, ultimately, unprofessional. However, it has sought to understand these states of mind and practices in their broader context. Professional leadership needs to address the various limiting contexts as much as the mindsets themselves. Before we end this part of the chapter we turn our attention to a dimension of organisational working that can be easily overlooked: the effects of the physical environment on professional social work.

The physical environment of organisations

The physical environment in which social work takes place usually reflects some of the other contextual factors that we have highlighted. For example, budget cuts, organisational structures and managerialism all influence the size, quality and layout of physical spaces in which social workers work. There is a strong relationship between our physical work environment and our mental and physical well-being (Hassard and Cox, undated). Depending on how the physical environment is designed, organised and resourced it can either promote or hinder professional leadership in social work. For example, practitioners need properly demarcated and safe spaces for downtime, critical reflection and (both formal and informal) professional discussions (UNISON, 2016). The lack of an appropriate working environment can also demonstrate the need for professional leadership, as the case study below will highlight.

Hot desk

Noun

- (In an office) a desk allocated to a worker when required or on a rota system, rather than belonging to a particular worker.

Verb

- Use a desk as required or on a rota system, rather than having one's own desk.

Oxford English Dictionary Online

Case study 4.3   Hotdesking can add to social worker stress

Hotdesking and poorly designed workplace environments can contribute to the stress on child and family social workers, according to a new study. Researchers at the Centre for Research on Children and Families found the lack of a desk for social workers to return

→

to after often difficult home visits added to their sense of 'emotional disorientation', left them without a physical 'secure base' to work from, and could reduce chances to interact with colleagues. The report said: 'Increasing uncertainty into a role, which is already dealing with high levels of uncertainty with their cases, will increase levels of stress. Reducing opportunities for working and meeting with colleagues takes away an important buffer of stress in this profession.'

The study, which involved a survey of 209 child and family social workers and a series of focus group interviews, looked at the determinants of stress and burnout. It concluded employers should prioritise improvements to workplace environments and support for individual social workers, after finding participants were often 'struggling with the demands of a large, complicated and ever changing workload' and facing high caseloads and paperwork. As well as hotdesking, other workplace factors found to have contributed to the emotional demands included noisy open plan offices, ineffective IT systems and practical issues such as the removal of parking near social work offices. Participants said each of these issues in themselves could potentially be overcome but the cumulative effect created an added strain on top of an already demanding job. Social workers frequently had to 'contain' their own emotional responses to the work they did with families experiencing distress and trauma, the study found. This took a lot of emotional [sic] and energy and was complicated by the 'every present tension' between protecting the child and acknowledging the distress of parents, it added.

Community Care, (2016a (abridged)

The research cited in the case study highlights how hotdesking and noisy open plan offices appear to make an already stressful role more difficult by denying social workers a 'secure base' to which they can return, gather their thoughts and reflect. It also highlights how office design can reflect management priorities over professional ones. For some social workers this seemed to exemplify a culture of inadequate support and not being listened to by management. In these circumstances it would be entirely understandable if practitioners did not feel valued in what they were doing, became demotivated and left their jobs as a consequence. Although, to their credit, many did not do that. Overall, the problems presented by hotdesking and open plan offices, together with other factors such as working in a blame culture, operating high caseloads and ineffective IT systems took an emotional toll and depleted energy.

The paradox of professional leadership

As has been discussed elsewhere in this chapter, in this research we see highlighted what could be described as the 'paradox of professional leadership' in social work. That is to say, the conditions that most require professional leadership are the ones that are most likely to deplete the mental energies of those involved and impair their willingness to involve themselves in leadership activities. When adverse working conditions threaten professionalism then leadership is required to make the argument, mobilise support and to push back or else things will not improve. In fact, they will deteriorate still further, with increasingly negative consequences for service users. While it is everyone's responsibility to fight for the profession, those on the frontline need support and leadership from leaders with a higher public profile and also from appropriate professional organisations. In this respect we note the efforts of Professor Eileen Munro (*Community Care*, 2016b), BASW (2015a) and UNISON (2016) on these very issues. All have campaigned to highlight the problem of social workers' working conditions. However, whether this has managed to remedy the problems is doubtful. Nevertheless, by bringing the issues into the public domain, it helps broaden the debate and increase the chances of developing appropriate strategies to effect positive change.

Factors that can limit the possibility of effective professional leadership: Summary of key points

- Social work takes place in a complex set of interrelated contexts: economic, political, financial, ideological, organisational, emotional and physical.

- Aspects of these contexts, on their own or in combination with others, can limit the possibilities of effective professional leadership taking place.

- This is because, among other things, they increase stress; contribute towards demotivation and burnout; reduce the possibilities for critical reflection and professional dialogues; deplete mental energy; and increase the likelihood of individual practitioners and teams becoming 'stuck' in a people-processing mentality and the practices that go along with that.

- The 'paradox of professional leadership' in social work is that the conditions that most require professional leadership are the ones that are most likely to deplete the mental energies of those involved.

- As a consequence, effective leadership needs to be able to identify such factors and find ways of combatting them. This is easier to do through collective and collaborative efforts within and across organisations.

Enabling factors in professional leadership in social work

In the previous section we discussed key macro and micro factors (individually and in combination) that can limit the possibilities of professional leadership taking place effectively in social work. In this section we look at factors that can promote or enable effective leadership. It might be reasonably assumed that professional leadership will be better enabled if the factors that we discussed previously are reversed, that is to say, if more resources are provided; social workers are given smaller caseloads; organisations are less managerialised; if there are better working environments; and so on. While that would be a fair starting assumption, and leadership in social work should be directed towards achieving those goals, there are other factors that can help promote professional leadership. We will focus more specifically on how practitioners can put professional leadership into practice in the following chapter. However, before we conclude this chapter, we highlight developments that can create a constructive context in which these practices can flourish.

Communities of Practice

Even though the activities to which it refers have gone on for centuries, the term 'Community (or Communities) of Practice' (CoP/CoPs) has come into circulation relatively recently. The concept is strongly associated with educational theorist Etienne Wenger (1998) and it has become widely discussed and adopted in health and social care (particularly nursing) since the 2000s (Le May, 2009).

According to Le May (ibid., p. 3) the best description of a community of practice is provided by Wenger, McDermott and Snyder (2002, pp. 4–5), who state that it is:

> *groups of people who share a concern, a set of problems, or a passion about a topic, and who deepen their understanding and knowledge of this area by interacting on an ongoing basis. … These people don't necessarily work together on a day-to-day basis, but they get together because they find value in their interactions. As they spend time together, they typically share information, insight, and advice. They solve problems. They help each other. They discuss their situation, their aspirations, their needs. They think about common issues. They explore ideas and act as sounding boards to each other. They may create tools, standards, generic designs, manuals, and other documents; or they may just keep what they know as a tacit understanding they share. … Over time, they develop a unique perspective on their topic as well as a body of common knowledge, practices, and approaches. They also develop personal relation-ships and established ways of interacting. They may even develop a common sense of identity. They become a community of practice.*

From this description, it should be fairly clear why CoPs can enable professional leadership in social work. As they involve the ongoing, collective sharing of ideas and concerns about subjects of common interest, they would appear to provide a constructive context for professional leadership for several reasons. By sharing ideas, insights and knowledge, CoPs play an important role in collective 'sense-making'. By providing a sounding board, they assist in the process of critical reflection, and they also help with creating a vision around which the profession can unite and therefore help strengthen professional identity. Because they are self-generating and motivated, they are driven both by a strong sense of values and of genuine commitment – all of which are important elements of professional leadership. They do not exist because of extrinsic factors such as legislation, policy or managerial dictates; they emerge out of shared interests and the desire to exchange ideas and knowledge.

Important features of CoPs are that they involve forming relationships *across* and *between* organisations. This not only helps with the cross-pollination of ideas and collective sense-making, it also helps prevent seeing social work as simply what one employing organisation does. Both of these features promote professional discourse. CoPs in social work need not just include professionally qualified social workers. It would be reasonable to expect that a range of stakeholders, especially service users, would be involved. For example, a CoP could form around areas such as adult safeguarding, mental health, palliative care, practice education or fostering. In these cases, the community concerned is strengthened by being multi-disciplinary and open to different perspectives. However, the main driver, whatever the group composition, would be the shared desire to improve practice.

CoPs: Some critical considerations

CoPs *per se* have not gained as much traction in social work as they have in areas such as nursing. However, there has been some critical commentary in areas where they have been adopted. Some studies (e.g. Kerno, 2008) have highlighted many of the constraints that we have already discussed. For example, CoPs can fail to function effectively due to constraints caused by lack of time, rigid organisational hierarchies and the lack of a shared culture of learning. Others (e.g. Probst and Borzillo, 2008) identified that CoPs failed, among other reasons, when there was a lack of a core group of actively engaged members; where there was a low level of one-to-one interaction between members (which is considered a key feature of CoPs); where there was a weak identification with the community; and where there was a reluctance to learn from others. Other critics have highlighted that the self-regulating nature of CoPs, which can be one of its chief strengths, can also be a cause of weakness if the community becomes too closed, too rigid and too narrow in its thinking. Rather than good practice, such CoPs can sustain suboptimal practices.

To summarise this discussion, it should be evident how, when functioning well, CoPs can provide a positive context and a good model for professional leadership in social work. The noteworthy factors about them are that they are interactive; they work between and across organisations; and they enable critical dialogue and collective sense-making. Thinking about CoPs continues to evolve (Le May, 2009). However, they are not the only form of network that can facilitate professional leadership.

Professional networks in social work

Networks and networking are important to social work for many reasons and we need to acquire and develop networking skills generally to be effective in practice (see Hardcastle, 2011, Chapter 10). We discuss further the use of networking skills in practice in Chapter 5. However, here we discuss the various types of professional network that exist.

'Professional network' is a loose description which encompasses organisations as diverse as the website *Linkedin* (https://uk.linkedin.com/) [which calls itself 'the world's largest professional network'] to local Rotary clubs and also to a whole variety of face-to-face and online groups and activities where professionals connect with each other for a common purpose. Beyond this broad aim, networks can differ greatly in their specific aims and objectives. Unlike CoPs, the connections need not be about learning or collective sense-making. However, a key feature of such networks is that they are not confined to people working in the same organisation. They operate across organisations and across geographical areas.

It has been highlighted elsewhere in this book that connectedness, relationships and collective dialogue, sense-making and knowledge exchange are all important for effective professional leadership. Therefore, social workers need to be aware of the networks that are available to them. Membership of such networks need not just be confined to professionally qualified and practising social workers; one would expect other stakeholders, such as service users, to be involved.

Activity 4.2   Researching professional networks

- Research what networks are available to you that could enable you to connect with others involved in social work so that you can exchange views and knowledge about social work issues and provide a sounding board for each other's ideas.
- They can be national, local, face-to-face or online.
- When you have a list, you could annotate it with some thoughts about such things as: size, composition of and criteria (if any) for membership; whether it is more about providing information or critical discussion; whether it campaigns (and if so on what sort of issues); what is its perspective?
- You might even add how you think it could be improved.

Commentary

The results will vary depending, to some extent, on where you are. While much can be found from the internet, some of the more local, informal networks might not be accessible through this means and might be available only through local directories and personal contacts.

Networks can range in how formally they are constituted. Sometimes they are kept going by word of mouth. Even though we are in the age of social media, do not take the lack of a web presence as necessarily meaning that networks do not exist.

Your research might have taken you back to discussions in Chapters 1 and 2 about social work as a profession. It might have prompted you to think: what actually counts as a 'professional' network? It possibly caused you to think about the ways in which a network talked about professionalism and about the meanings of what 'professional' is that lay beneath any discussions. For example, in mental health you might have a network involving professionally qualified practitioners only where discussions focus primarily on clinical issues and are framed within psychiatric or psychological discourse. Conversely, there might be networks that are run by mental health service users to which practitioners are invited. Here the discourse would be less psychiatric and concepts like 'recovery' might be more in the foreground. Both networks might consider themselves committed to improving 'patient care' in mental health but have different perspectives on what that means and how it can be achieved. This indicates that it is probably useful to be part of more than one network. This will protect against insularity and even groupthink.

There are national networks of various kinds. Some are primarily professional networks; others provide networking opportunities as part of a range of functions. Some well-known examples that social workers should know about are listed below. Apart from their own websites they have a presence on various social media platforms, which are often where much of the online networking takes place.

British Association of Social Workers (BASW)

We discussed BASW and the role it plays in professional social work in Chapter 2. It describes itself as:

> *the largest professional association for social work in the UK, with offices in England, Northern Ireland, Scotland and Wales. We're here to promote the best possible social work services for all people who may need them, while also securing the well-being of social workers.*

Social Work Action Network (SWAN)

We also discussed SWAN in Chapter 2. It describes itself as:

> *a radical, campaigning organisation of social work and social care practitioners, students, service users, carers and academics, united by our concern that social work practice is being undermined by managerialism and marketization, by the stigmatisation of service users and by welfare cuts and restrictions.*

> http://www.socialworkfuture.org/

UNISON

UNISON is a public services trade union which many social workers join. As well as services for its members such as education, advice and support, it has a record of campaigning for social work and it also enables social work members to blog about social work via its website.

https://www.unison.org.uk/

The Social Care Institute for Excellence (SCIE)

SCIE describes itself as: 'a leading improvement support agency and an independent charity working with adults', families' and children's care and support services across the UK'.

Its primary function is more about sharing knowledge rather than networking *per se*. However, it does enable networking opportunities either formally (e.g. The Co-production Network) or informally by providing information about and contacts for projects that can be followed up.

www.scie.org.uk/index

Guardian social care network

The Guardian social care network is part of *the Guardian* Professional Networks, which describes itself as: 'a collection of community sites that bring professionals together to share ideas, celebrate success and explore the challenges they face in their working lives'.

https://www.theguardian.com/social-care-network

Community Care

Like *the Guardian*, *Community Care* is run by a media company. It enables networking for its readers and subscribers who are involved in social work. (http://www.communitycare.co.uk/)

Either on its own or in collaboration with organisations such as BASW and UNISON, *Community Care* organises campaigns and provides both online and face-to-face/conference opportunities for professional networking.

Finally, for those working in affiliated organisations, Research in Practice (https://www.rip.org.uk/) and Research in Practice for Adults (https://www.ripfa.org.uk/) provide research knowledge and networking opportunities across different areas of social work.

Summary: The importance of networks for professional leadership

This discussion of networks has been brief. Nevertheless, it indicates the diverse range of networking opportunities to which social workers can connect to inform themselves about, exchange views on and make sense of developments that affect professional social work. The presence of such networks and, where they exist, CoPs is a vital element of professional leadership for this reason.

CoPs and professional networks of various kinds are therefore both enabling factors in making professional leadership more likely to happen. However, they are also the result of the professional leadership which started them and keeps them going. Social workers who are connected and in active discussion with other social work practitioners and stakeholders in social work are better placed to perform effective leadership roles than those who are isolated and struggling to make sense of the issues on their own. Being connected to networks is also an effective means of helping to build resilience (Grant and Kinman, 2014), which is important for leadership as we will discuss further in Chapter 5.

As we have discussed at various times in earlier chapters, social workers can struggle with developing a strong and clear professional identity. Professional leadership is more difficult if we lack a sense of who we are professionally and what our purpose is as social workers. Connectedness with others – both within and outside our employing organisations – is an important way of establishing a stronger professional identity.

Learning organisations

We have discussed throughout the book how features of organisations can militate against professional leadership taking place effectively. For example, we have highlighted the challenges faced when working in organisations that are rigidly bureaucratic, hierarchical and managerialised. Partly in recognition of these stifling factors, attempts have been made in recent decades to create organisational cultures which positively facilitate creativity, innovation, leadership and, above all, the ability to learn (see, for example, Argyris and Schön, 1978; Eraut, 1994).

The particular term 'learning organisation' is associated with the American systems scientist Peter Senge (1990). According to Senge organisations are dynamic systems in states of continuous adaptation. However, while, theoretically, they have the potential for improving performance, much of the time many organisations do not make improvements very easily in practice. Senge observed that most efforts to change are hampered by resistance created by practices that have become part of the organisational culture – usually to such an extent that the management system on its own is often powerless to do anything about it.

A 'learning organisation' requires the organisation as a whole to be able to look at itself, to identify problems, learn from experience and adapt continuously to changing external conditions. This requires all the organisation's systems (e.g. management, HR, frontline, back room, administrative and so on) to join up effectively and feedback to each other usable information that enables meaningful learning to take place – the end goal being an improvement of the quality of the service.

In social work, learning organisations are strongly advocated to enable and support critical, reflexive, humane and evidence-based practice as well as continuous professional development (CPD) (Higham, 2009; White, 2013; Field and Brown, 2016). The SCIE developed an audit tool to enable social care organisations to assess whether they meet the criteria for a learning organisation. They also provide information and resources for those bodies which want to become one (SCIE, 2008). Much of it is about having systems in place to gather meaningful feedback from all stakeholders, but particularly service users. It also requires internal systems to be responsive to any changes required and to be able to identify and meet staff development needs. An important part of this in social work is having a system of good quality supervision (SCIE, 2012), which will be discussed further in the next chapter.

While many social work organisations aspire to be learning organisations and have various service user feedback mechanisms in place and also commitments to CPD, the reality is one of patchy achievements in practice, particularly if the main criterion of success is improvement to the quality of the service. This can largely be explained by reference to the factors discussed earlier in the chapter. It remains one of the goals of professional leadership for social work organisations to become learning organisations as actually conceptualised by theorists such as Argyris, Schön and Senge, rather than be the sites of thwarted ambitions in this respect.

Chapter summary

....

- CoPs and professional networks of all kinds help connect social workers to each other and to other stakeholders in social work. They mainly work across and between organisations rather than being confined to within single organisations. This promotes the exchange of knowledge and ideas, helps provide a sounding board on important issues, enables sense-making, helps build resilience and contributes to establishing a clear and stronger professional identity. All these factors make professional leadership more likely to take place.
- Many private and public organisations aspire to become 'learning organisations' whereby they endeavour to improve their performance on a systemic basis. When such feedback and staff development systems work well, organisations can not only mitigate the negative effects of factors such as rigid hierarchies and managerialism, they can also enable the conditions under which professional leadership is more likely to be effective.
- Professional leadership not only benefits from professional networks of various kinds and from learning cultures in organisations, it also needs to actively promote them.

Further reading

Community Care (2016b) Munro: 'Hotdesking is harming social work'. Available online at:http://www.communitycare.co.uk/2016/04/29/munro-hotdesking-harming-social-work/

This is an interesting article on the effects of hotdesking on social workers.

Community Care (2017c) Social workers working through illness to keep up with caseloads. Available online at: http://www.communitycare.co.uk/2017/07/17/social-workers-working-illness-keep-caseloads/

Ferguson, H (2014) Is your social work 'dead' or 'alive'? The gap between inspiring and defensive practice. Harry Ferguson's opening speech at JSWEC. Available online at: http://www.communitycare.co.uk/2014/07/23/social-work-dead-alive-difference-inspiring-defensive-practice/

Ferguson shares findings from his research observing social workers about how their practice came to be 'dead' (automated/defensive) or 'alive' (inspiring/engaged).

The Guardian (2017a) Children's social care services 'set to reach breaking point'. *The Guardian*, 11 May. Available online at: https://www.theguardian.com/society/2017/may/11/childrens-social-care-services-set-to-reach-breaking-point

This article explains how funding for children's social care services is not keeping up with demand and the effect this is having both on social workers and service users.

Le May, A (2009) (ed.) *Communities of practice in health and social care*. Chichester: Wiley-Blackwell.

This provides a good exposition of the concept of 'communities of practice' and how they relate to health and social care services.

McFadden, P (2015) *Measuring burnout among UK social workers*. Sutton: Community Care.

This study explains the concept of 'burnout' in social work and shares findings into its causes.

SCIE (2008) *Learning organisations: Key characteristics*. Available online at:https://www.scie.org.uk/publications/learningorgs/key/index.asp

This SCIE resource explains more about the concept of the 'learning organisation' in the context of social care.

UNISON (2015) UNISON joins social work campaign. Available online at: https://www.unison.org.uk/news/article/2015/08/unison-joins-social-work-campaign/

5: Putting Professional Leadership Into Practice

Achieving a social work degree

This chapter will enable you to develop the following capabilities to the appropriate level from the PCF:

- knowledge
- critical reflection and analysis
- intervention and skills
- contexts and organisations
- professional leadership
- professionalism.

It will also introduce you to the following academic standards as set out in the social work subject benchmark statement:

5.2 Social Work theory
5.3 Values and ethics
5.4 Service users and carers
5.5 The nature of Social Work practice, in the UK and more widely
5.6 The leadership, organisation and delivery of Social Work services
5.10 Problem-solving skills
5.15 Communication skills
5.16 Skills in working with others
5.17 Skills in personal and professional development

(Continued)

(Continued)

More specifically it will enable you to:

- use the concept of the 'incomplete leader' to understand how collective and situational models of professional leadership can be applied to social work practice;
- understand how professional leadership is conceptualised in professional social work guidance;
- reflect critically on the skills, qualities and knowledge required by leaders and followers in putting professional leadership into practice in social work;
- reflect how professional socialisation influences practice, particularly through role-modelling and formal and informal supervision.

Introduction

In Chapters 3 and 4 we discussed how the concept of leadership has a range of possible meanings, with various models in circulation. This highlighted that there is no agreed single way of how to 'do' leadership. However, it was proposed that, to be effective and in line with professional guidance, professional leadership in social work should most appropriately draw on collective and situational models. In this conceptualisation, individuals adopt various leadership roles and undertake different leadership tasks, contributing as and when the situation requires it (Davies and Ross, 2016). Leadership is therefore not just the preserve of managers. We also highlighted the importance of the leader–follower relationship and importance of the role played by followers generally in enabling effective leadership to take place. Leadership roles in social work might therefore include tasks as diverse as information and opinion giver, sense-maker and clarifier, knowledge seeker, knowledge imparter, advice provider, direction giver, teacher of skills, communication facilitator, problem solver, tension reliever, participation encourager and so on. Followers can also play an active leadership role when the situation requires it, such as seeking clarification, giving moral support and energy, being receptive, questioning, giving constructive criticism, actively participating in discussions and so on.

The list of all potential roles involved in leadership and followership is extensive, making the task of unpacking them in terms of the necessary skills, knowledge and attributes required impossible in one chapter. Therefore, to make this task manageable in ways that incorporate core leadership roles, we return to the four broad leadership capabilities set out by Ancona et al. (2007). These are: 'sense-making'; 'relating'; 'visioning'; and 'inventing'. We examine the skills and qualities required to be effective in these areas as well as providing examples of this happening in social work. We then turn to what current professional guidance expects in terms of professional leadership practice and focus particularly on the importance of role-modelling and supervision in different forms.

The chapter includes both case studies and activities which are designed not only to demonstrate professional leadership in practice, but also to encourage you to think about your own leadership strengths and areas for development. The chapter concludes with a summary of key points, together with suggestions for further reading in selected areas.

The 'incomplete leader'

In 'In praise of the incomplete leader', Ancona et al. (ibid.) argue that leadership is a collective effort based upon four leadership capabilities that all organisations need. The capabilities are:

- sense-making – interpreting developments;
- relating – building trusting relationships;
- visioning – communicating a compelling image of the future;
- inventing – coming up with new ways of doing things.

Sense-making

The idea of sense-making in professional and organisational contexts is strongly associated with the American organisational theorist Karl Weick (1995). Broadly speaking, it is the process by which people in organisations come together to understand the various things that affect their working lives. This includes any new, unexpected or potentially confusing developments experienced collectively. Weick argues that sense-making is basically a social activity in that it involves people having conversations and dialogues with each other during which they exchange plausible narratives about what they believe is happening and why. As people communicate with each other and develop their narratives it helps them to organise their thoughts, process their experiences and create a meaningful order out of all the things that are happening. The process is more about establishing a shared understanding of what is going on rather than discovering the 'truth' of the matter. Importantly, in order to maximise nuance, subtlety and precision of understanding, Weick advises 'do whatever you can to increase the variety of the language with which you work' (ibid., p. 196). This suggests that, as social workers, we should not only try to widen our range of reading and broaden our personal and professional vocabulary, but also to be more expressive and precise in how we communicate with each other. Weick also believed that a person or group's sense of who they are (their identity) is an important factor in shaping how they interpret events. This suggests that the more we work on our professionalism as social workers the more professional our sense-making will be.

Activity 5.1 provides the opportunity both to explore the importance of sense-making in professional leadership and to consider the skills and qualities needed to contribute effectively to this process.

Activity 5.1 Sense-making in social work

At any given time in social work there are concepts, agendas, events, policies and other new developments that need to be made sense of in order to be able to practise professionally. It is not professional for social workers to just wait passively until someone else tells them what the implications are. Part of being professional and part of practising professional leadership is to think for ourselves and to actively try to understand what is happening currently and what is coming down the line in the future. It is also about being able to understand the broader context in which developments take place.

At the time of writing there are a whole range of different events, policies and developments that either have or will have implications for social work of some form or another. They include:

- the introduction of a new social work regulator;
- the introduction of the Children and Social Work Act 2017;
- the introduction of Universal Credit;
- debates about female genital mutilation (FGM);
- continued concern about how best to support unaccompanied asylum seekers;
- 'Brexit';
- the concept of 'mentalisation' in relation to assessing attachment;
- the concept of 'co-production' in relation to adult social care;
- the funding of adult social care;
- the 'crisis' in mental health services;
- social work apprenticeships.

Task

Choose a topic either from the list or one that is more relevant at the time of reading. As this list indicates, it can be a new piece of legislation, policy, concept or event that will have direct or indirect implications for social work.

- Explain how you would make sense of that topic in a way that helps you understand its relevance to social work.
- What skills and qualities would you need in order to have a constructive dialogue with others about what it meant for social work?
- Why might professional leadership be needed in this area?

Commentary

There are various ways of making sense of these topics. It is always a good idea to seek many types and sources of data. An obvious starting point is to access reputable journalistic sources such as *The Guardian* and *Community Care*. Academic journals are useful, of course, but there can often be a time lag between issues emerging and academic analysis being published. Official explanations can be found on the relevant government websites. Professional perspectives can be gained from organisations such as BASW, SWAN or UNISON. Service user perspectives can be gathered from various national and local sources. Gathering a range of perspectives is important, but we still need to process the information we have. It might have gaps, it might be biased and it still might not be clear what the implications are for your particular area of social work. This is where critical reflection, exchange of views and dialogue with others is useful. This helps the process of putting things into their wider context, of assessing what is relevant, what is fact and what is opinion and establishing not only what the immediate implications are, but also what the wider significance of any development is. This process needs to be ongoing because any potential impact can change over time.

In the first instance, do not assume you already know what is going on or what the situation is. The most important quality to have is an open and inquiring mind and professional curiosity. We not only need to be interested in gathering professional knowledge, but also knowledge about social and political issues and current affairs generally. Asking questions (and clarifying what we do not know) is as important for leadership as providing solutions. It also helps greatly if the complexities, subtleties and nuances of any issue can be appreciated. We always need to beware of lapsing into stereotypes. Beyond developing this mindset, the key skills needed are: the ability to reflect critically; to be able to put things in their appropriate context; to be able to analyse; and to be able to assess information for relevance and evaluate it for accuracy. In order to have constructive dialogues with others we need to be able to communicate effectively. This means listening respectfully (but not uncritically) to others' opinions. It also means being able to express ourselves clearly and in ways that mean that others can understand our message (with all its nuances). In this respect Ancona (2005) suggests the use of images, metaphors and stories can improve the communication of critical elements. As has been discussed elsewhere, an important element of leadership is the ability to influence others. In this respect we need to have integrity and honesty in our dealings.

In answering the final question, it clearly depends on what the issue or topic is. While specific legislation and policy targeted at social work have direct impact, other developments such as changes in government economic and social policy can play out in a variety of ways that impact on social work. But this might not be immediately obvious. The leadership challenge is to understand what the implications are both for the profession and its service users, and to work out appropriate responses that are in line with professional values and that fit with the roles of social work. Simply to rely on what is said in governmental or managerial statements – where they exist – is not enough. You need to be able to critique from a professional standpoint. This is particularly relevant when you consider what was said about social work being concerned much of the time with 'wicked problems'. As Weick (1995, p. 34) observed, complexity requires a 'complex sensing system'.

When agreed courses of action are apparent then another important task of professional leadership is for the profession to inform itself of best practice in that area. This is where guidance such as the PCF and KSSs become an important reference point in our own learning and also in helping others to learn. There are several ways that this can be done in organisations, including, as stated in the PCF, practice research, supervision, assessment of practice, teaching and management.

Relating

The second leadership capability we consider is 'relating'. Ancona et al. (2007) broke this down into: building trusting relationships, balancing advocacy (explaining your viewpoints) with enquiry (listening to understand others' viewpoints) and cultivating networks of supportive confidants. None of these activities requires a special 'leadership' skillset or mindset; they are all core social work skills and reflect social work values (Stewart, Clarke and Lishman, 2009; Hardcastle, 2011; Mantell, 2013; Parker and Doel, 2013; Davies and Jones, 2016). This provides another illustration of how, in large part, professional leadership should not be regarded as involving capabilities that require special qualities over and beyond those needed in professional social work practice generally. The skills of relationship building, communication, advocacy and networking form a core part of normal social work practice and should be developed and built upon throughout a social worker's career. You will find these core skills covered in most social work practice skills texts (for example, Parker and Bradley, 2014; Davies and Jones, 2016; and so on). However, the remaining two capabilities listed by Ancona et al. (2007) are probably less well covered in mainstream social work texts and require a fuller discussion.

Visioning

According to Ancona et al. (ibid., p. 92) 'visioning' is about 'creating credible and compelling images of a desired future that people in the organization want to create together'. On the face of it, this particular task might appear to be beyond the capabilities or remit of individual students and social practitioners. 'Visioning' is not a concept covered in professional social work guidance, nor, for that matter, in most social work textbooks. However, that does not mean that it is not extremely relevant to social work, whether this be in strategic planning at organisational level or everyday practice with service users.

First, we need to remember that, in the context of professional leadership in social work, visioning is best conceived as a collective activity. Therefore, visions will emerge from conversations between colleagues and consultations with colleagues and others involved in social work. Opportunities for such conversations actually occur quite frequently, often given impetus by organisations such as BASW or UNISON. For example, the UK Standing Conference for Social Work and Social Workers, hosted by BASW, was set up by a wide range of social work organisations precisely in order to seek 'a shared view of the challenges and opportunities for social work' (*The Guardian*, 2017b). Therefore, visioning is a very important activity in order to be able to develop social work in ways that enable the profession to meet the many challenges it faces. How social work will develop in the future should be something that engages everyone involved with social work – but especially social workers themselves. Social work cannot allow itself to be defined by others, whether this be by the government of the day, other professions or the media.

Second, visioning need not be about the future of the whole of social work; it can be about a particular service or branch of a service such as children's social care, adoption, adult social work, care homes, social work education and so on. It can also be about how a particular local organisation or service should be run. A search online will soon show reports and other documents claiming to offer a 'vision' for some aspect of social work or social care. However, any particular vision needs to be informed by a broader sense of what professional social work is about more generally and where that specific service fits into the bigger picture.

Lastly, whatever theoretical approach is adopted, a fundamental task of social work practice is working with others to produce desired change (Parker and Bradley, 2014; Payne, 2014). It is hard to see how change can realistically be expected to take place without having 'a credible and compelling image of a desired future' (Ancona et al., 2007, p. 92). While working with service users and others to create images of what might and what should happen in the future is very seldom referred to as 'visioning' in practice (we might, for example, use more accessible terms like 'hypothesising', 'planning' and 'goalsetting', for example), the principle is the same. Creating a credible image of what we want to aim for helps motivate and guide us to go forward to something better. Therefore, initiating and contributing to such conversations with service users and others (i.e. 'visioning') is actually what social workers do as part of their everyday practice.

To conclude, visioning, in some form or another and whatever language is used, is an important social work activity in many spheres. Just as we need to be able to enable service users to vision for their own future well-being and that of their families, so the social work profession needs to be able to create compelling and credible visions of its own future and for all those whom it serves. To do this effectively clearly requires the ability to reflect upon, analyse and read the current situation, but also a degree of imagination and the ability to project ahead and anticipate trends in the future. Again, this would be more effectively done collectively rather than as an individual. Wenger (1998) argued that imagination was an important element that enabled communities of practice to form and flourish. Connecting with the experiences of other practitioners, service users and carers, and learning about other situations, helps stimulate our imagination by gaining new perspectives and opening up new possibilities. As well as creating new visions, an important function of professional leadership is to constantly assess whether the current vision is fit for purpose and appropriate to the challenges it faces or whether it needs to be revised (re-visioned) in some way.

Case study 5.1   *Transforming children and young people's mental health provision*

In 2017, the Government (via the Department of Health and Department for Education) published a Green Paper on *Transforming children and young people's mental health provision* (H.M. Government, 2017). A Green Paper can be seen as a form of visioning exercise undertaken by the government. A Green Paper usually sets out various policy proposals on a specific topic in order to stimulate discussion. The aim of Green Papers is to get feedback from specific stakeholders but also from the public at large. Green Papers normally contain several alternative policies for review before a final decision is made. A Green Paper usually leads to a more focused White Paper, which clarifies and confirms the policy vision which will form the basis for future legislation.

As part of the consultation process, the government enabled children and young people to contribute via an online consultation process. However, reacting to the fact that the Green Paper made no mention of social work, BASW issued the following statement on its website:

> BASW welcomes the Government's focus on mental health services for children and young people, but is dissatisfied by the omission of social workers from the Green Paper. The mental health needs of children and young people is something that impacts on all children's social workers, whether they are working with children in the care system, children in the criminal justice system, children living with their families, children with disabilities, young carers, unaccompanied asylum-seeking children and care leavers. It is therefore a surprise that social workers and Children and Adolescent Mental Health Services are not acknowledged formally within the document. The paper also refers to mental health support teams, but provides little insight into how these would operate. Social workers are fundamental in working with other professionals within such a supportive multi-disciplinary remit and it is important the balance of these teams is not dominated by the NHS or a 'medical model' and incorporates social models too. Social workers have the essential knowledge and holistic understanding of how frontline services function, as well as skills and experience in direct work and must absolutely be recognised as part of the solution. BASW will issue a fuller response after consultation with our members.
>
> BASW, 2017

Questions

1.   Do you think that children and young people's mental health provision is an area where social work plays a role and might have an appropriate contribution to make in thinking about both policy and practice? Give reasons.

⟶

2. Comment on the professional leadership shown by BASW generally. More specifically, explain why visioning could be considered to be an important part of this.

3. If you practised in this specific area what knowledge, skills and qualities would you need to be able to contribute effectively to this consultation process?

Commentary

As the statement by BASW indicates, working with (and therefore knowing about) the mental health of children and young people is an important part of much social work practice. Social workers are important members of multi-disciplinary teams working in this area. Social workers therefore have a great deal of experience and expertise in this sphere. As BASW suggests, their perspective will be different from that of their health colleagues. For these reasons it would be very appropriate to include a social work perspective in a consultation about service provision.

BASW have demonstrated professional leadership by acting to respond appropriately to the government's omission by making a submission on behalf of professional social work. As professional leaders they initiated a consultation process giving members the opportunity to contribute. They therefore alerted their membership to the fact that the Green Paper had been published and then encouraged them to take appropriate action. Even though they were apparently not 'in the loop' of designated consultation stakeholders, BASW made sure that a social work perspective would be offered even though it might not be accepted. Visioning is important in this process because BASW needs to offer more than just an accumulation of responses from various individuals, some of them possibly negative. In order to be effective, it needs to create a 'credible and compelling image' as Ancona et al. (2007) would say. From the collective contributions of its membership BASW needs to create a coherent vision of what children and young people's mental health provision should look like from a social work perspective.

Any practitioner who works in a branch of social work that involves children and young people's mental health should be able to make an appropriate professional contribution to such a consultation. However, first you would need to know that the consultation existed. You cannot take for granted that your employing organisation will know or pass this information on to you if it does. This underlines the importance of being networked. You have a much better chance of knowing about any developments if you are a member of a professional body or network or, at least, follow relevant organisations on social media. Therefore, you need to be proactive and be on top of policy statements coming out of government that affect your area of social work. In terms of knowledge, you would need to know how the current system operated and what changes were being proposed. You would then need to reflect critically in order to be able to understand (make sense of) the possible implications for social workers, service users and the system generally. Sense-making would be easier if it was part of a wider conversation with others. The ability to communicate effectively and work well in collaboration with others is therefore important. You would then be able to create a credible vision of your preferred option. This would be greatly strengthened by being supported by a range of appropriate knowledge. A vision need not be created from nothing; you might want to add to or amend a vision already in existence. Finally, you would also need to be able to argue your case effectively. That is to say, to gather evidence and communicate sufficiently skilfully to get your vision across and, ideally, influence decision-making. In this respect, using appropriate media to bring it into the public domain might prove useful. None of this would necessarily be done as an individual (even though it could be). A submission produced collectively, appropriately evidenced and delivered in an appropriately professional manner would carry more weight.

Summary

Much that has been written about visioning skills in the context of leadership focuses on the role of transformational leaders and others at the top of business organisations. However, being able to vision should be regarded as a transferable skill that also applies to practising professional leadership in social work. Visioning is closely allied to sense-making. Combined, they are about making sense of what has happened in the past and what is happening currently and then creating a picture of what we think could and *should* happen in the future. We need to have a certain degree of imagination to vision. However as was discussed above, the skills most required to vision are those of reflection, hypothesising, interpretation and analysis, which are all core social work capabilities (BASW, 2018b). Also, in some areas of leadership studies, although much is talked about visioning in terms of 'blue skies thinking' or 'thinking outside the box', we should not be deterred from visioning by the obligation to come up with something completely original. Some of the best visions can develop from research into existing developments in other areas and be adapted to our particular situation (see 'Inventing' below). So, again, this underlines not only the value of professional imagination and curiosity, but also research-mindedness, problem-solving skills and the ability to be solution-focused rather than dazzlingly original *per se*. There is often truth in the old cliché that there is no need to reinvent the wheel.

Inventing

According to Ancona et al. (2007, p. 92) inventing means 'creating new ways of approaching tasks or overcoming seemingly insurmountable problems to turn visions into reality'. In the context of professional leadership in social work inventing might be better conceptualised as innovative or problem-solving practice. However, whatever terms we use, inventing is crucial if professional social work is to develop and move forward. It is a key leadership capability. It is also important for the future of social work that innovation comes from within the profession itself (preferably in dialogue with service users) rather than to have new ideas and practices imposed from government and other outside sources (Templeton, 2016). As with all the capabilities, putting inventing into practice effectively requires a certain professional mindset, together with a mixture of qualities, knowledge and skills. We can best start to unpack these by discussing the case study below.

Case study 5.2   Social Worker of the Year Awards. Yasmin Ishaq: Creative and Innovative Social Work Practice. Implementing peer-supported open dialogue

The Social Worker of the Year Awards were established in 2006 by the social worker, Beverley Williams (www.socialworkawards.com). Arguably, the founding of the awards is a very good example of professional leadership in itself. In the context of professional leadership in social work it is worth finding out more about the different award categories and what past winners achieved their awards for. Helen Pye, who won the Overall Social Worker of the Year and Mental Health Social Worker of the Year awards in 2015, and Carolyne Willow, who won the award for Championing Social Work Values in 2017, are particularly good examples of practitioners championing social work in what might have been considered unfavourable circumstances, but all of the different award winners are worth reading about. It could well serve to stimulate your own imagination about what is possible. However, the extract below focuses on the 2016 winner for Creative and Innovative Social Work Practice, Yasmin Ishaq.

In a quarter-century social work career, Yasmin has been no stranger to developing and delivering new services. Over the past year, her focus has turned to implementing peer-supported open dialogue – based on a mental health treatment model originating in Finland – in Kent. It involves maintaining a consistent relationship with a service user's family and social network, by the same practitioners throughout their care, with all decisions being co-created by the client, their support system and professionals. Crisis interventions within 24 hours are designed to keep people from hospital admissions wherever possible, and by drawing on family and community resources the aim is to reduce reliance on traditional services and medication. Judges praised the work as 'genuinely innovative', pointing out that Yasmin is the only social worker in the country who's leading in this area – more commonly the territory of medical professionals. A family member of one service user who's been involved in the project simply describes her as 'epitomising the word "hope"'.

Social Worker of the Year Awards, 2016

→

Task

1. Check out more about this award by following the link.
2. What are your thoughts about this story?
3. In what ways might Yasmin Ishaq have demonstrated the leadership capability of 'inventing'?
4. Reflect on what led her to be innovative and what enabled her to be effective in what she did.

Commentary

In some respects, the main features of peer-supported open dialogue (e.g. adopting practice that is consistent, relationship-focused, strengths-based and working in partnership) might not seem that original to someone familiar with social work. Yasmin did not invent these approaches to practice. The innovative bit was, first, finding that this method of working was effective elsewhere (Finland) and, second, introducing it to an area of service delivery in this country which is traditionally dominated by medical perspectives. The case study shows that inventing does not have to involve starting with a blank piece of paper. It can be about introducing a technique or method from one area to another or one service to another.

This innovation in practice appears to have been driven by Yasmin's professional curiosity to explore new ideas and by her commitment to social work values. She did not appear to have a formal leadership role in the organisation at the start of the process. However, Yasmin was not content simply to maintain the status quo in the way the service in which she worked was delivered. This was particularly because it did not seem to fully embody social work principles. Yasmin was not afraid to 'go out on a limb' and try something different. She used her initiative and found something which she believed to be useful to her work in mental health with children and young people. The method that she found was not only supported by a body of evidence, it also reflected social work values better than the existing system. Therefore, much of Yasmin's professional leadership in this case was having a mindset that did not automatically accept the status quo and showed professional curiosity and research-mindedness to look for something better. Importantly, it also reflected a strong sense of the contribution that contemporary social work can make.

Once the method of peer-supported open dialogue had been identified and found to be relevant to her line of work, Yasmin would have also needed to be able to communicate her ideas effectively and argue her case sufficiently cogently to influence those with the power to agree to bring in the new model. The Lead Psychologist for East Kent Secondary Care and Open Dialogue, James Osborne, is quoted as saying:

> *Yasmin was instrumental in drawing the organisation's awareness to this innovative treatment in mental health and has showed the tenacity required to bring about something new in an organisation when financial pressures loom heavy over the quality agenda.*

> Ibid.

In summary, we see that Yasmin demonstrated a range of skills and qualities in bringing in this innovation. This included use of initiative, professional curiosity, research-mindedness, communication and the ability to influence. However, it is worth noting that, over and above those that we have mentioned, she was also commended for her tenacity, especially in unfavourable conditions. Tenacity, commitment and resilience are very important but undervalued qualities in social work practice generally (Edmonson, 2013), but very important qualities in leadership.

Remember the point of the incomplete leader

It is possible to see elements of all four of the leadership capabilities combined in this case study. However, remember that the main thrust of the argument put forward by Ancona et al. (2007) was that no single leader can be strong in every department. All leaders are incomplete in some way or another. Also remember that, based on the argument of these writers and others, we spent most of Chapter 3 arguing that professional leadership in social work should be conceived not only as a collective activity, but also one that, to be effective, requires the active participation of followers in the process. Therefore, it might be tempting to read the case study above as evidence that professional leadership comes down to the actions of individuals with exceptional skills and qualities. While there is no doubt that there are many exceptional people involved in social work, social work is too broad an activity and one that faces too many complex challenges for its professional leadership to be left to a small minority of individuals, however exceptional they may be.

As we have highlighted throughout, we need to take the responsibility to lead as necessary, but we cannot all be leaders all of the time. We might need to be prepared to adopt an appropriate follower role much of the time. However, the fact remains that we also need to take the responsibility to play a leadership role when the situation requires it. This suggests that, when it comes to inventing – as with all the capabilities – we need to think about the leader–follower relationship and the contributions we can make both as a leader and as a follower. In this respect, it would be useful to reflect on how Yasmin Ishaq's colleagues possibly enabled her to introduce the open dialogue model. Did they encourage her, did they listen to her ideas and make suggestions, did they help with the research or with influencing management or did they ignore her and block her at every turn? That can only be a matter of speculation here, but it underlines what has already been said about working in organisations: some climates are more conducive to change and more open to new ideas than others (Adair, 2009a). As followers we can help mitigate the effects of a negative organisational context by being constructive in our comments, supportive of each other's efforts and generally helping to create a positive climate.

The final exercise in this section will enable you to reflect more on where you are at the moment, but also what more you could do to develop yourself both as a leader and as a follower.

Activity 5.2

1. Consider the four leadership capabilities: sense-making; relating; visioning; and inventing. What roles can followers play to ensure that they support these activities effectively?
2. Reflect on the extent to which you currently have the necessary skills and qualities to practise the different leadership capabilities, but also the supporting followership roles.
3. What are your strengths and what are your priorities for development?

Commentary

There are many roles that followers can play in all of the leadership capabilities. In Chapter 3 we discussed Kelley's (1988) typology of followers in which he states that characteristics of effective followers are that they think for themselves and carry out their duties and assignments with energy and assertiveness. He goes on to say that 'because they are risk takers, self-starters, and independent problem solvers, [effective followers] they get consistently high ratings from peers and many superiors' (ibid., p. 145). We also referenced two concepts from Grint (2010): those of constructive dissent and destructive assent. Therefore, in general terms, effective followers need to be able to think for themselves and be prepared to offer construct criticism to leaders, even if this is constructive dissent. They cannot allow themselves to become sheep, 'yes men' or alienated. Another important role that followers can play, even if they are struggling to help significantly with making sense, visioning or inventing, is to try to maintain group morale, assist with promoting resilience and bring energy to the group. As we have discussed, leadership can falter under circumstances such as fatigue, stress, burnout or cynicism. Nurturing skills are therefore important, which might mean providing words of encouragement, offering to send out for coffee and cakes while the team engages in some difficult problem-solving or lightening the mood with humour. Collective leadership requires that leaders and followers take responsibility and contribute what they can. They need to be aware of and validate the contributions of others. If your skillset is more group-focused than task-focused, then playing to your strengths will enable others to play to theirs.

Responses to questions 2 and 3 will inevitably vary from individual to individual. However, as has been highlighted throughout the book, many of the foundation skills and qualities required for both effective leadership and followership – for example communication, relationship building, critical reflection, analytical thinking, networking, resilience, tenacity and so on – are the core skills of social work. What has been flagged up as particularly important for leadership is professional curiosity, the ability to situate social work in context and understand the bigger picture, as well the willingness to take the initiative, be proactive and to be creative.

Making sense of professional leadership in professional guidance

The previous section used the model provided by Ancona et al. (2007) to discuss how core leadership capabilities of sense-making, relating, visioning and inventing relate to social work. In this section we turn our attention to how professional leadership is conceived in contemporary guidance for professional social work. In previous chapters it was explained how the requirement to demonstrate professional leadership came to be embedded in professional social work guidance, particularly the PCF. You could argue that definitions of professional leadership contained in contemporary professional guidance should be the main, if not exclusive, focus of this chapter. However, we need to bear in mind the lessons of Chapter 2. Professional guidance is constantly changing in line with many different factors, including evolving ideas about social work generally. Although it is obviously important to be up to date, it is also wise not to become uncritically wedded to what is contained in specific guidance provided at any one time. In fact, to underline this very point, in Chapter 4 it was noted that, six years after it was introduced, the PCF was refreshed in 2018, with professional leadership significantly reconceptualised as a broader set of activities from those described in the original version. The final revised description concerning professional leadership in the PCF is reproduced below (BASW, 2018b).

> *We develop and show our leadership, individually and collectively, through promoting social work's purpose, practices and impact. We achieve this through diverse activities which may include: advancing practice; supervising; educating others; research; evaluation; using innovation and creativity; writing; using social media positively; being active in professional networks and bodies; contributing to policy; taking formal leadership/management roles. We promote organisational contexts conducive to good practice and learning. We work in partnership with people who use services and stake-holders in developing our leadership and aims for the profession.*

Leadership necessary in creating the right context for good practice to flourish

The overarching message contained in this statement is that the purpose of professional leadership is 'promoting social work's purpose, practices and impact'. The statement enumerates several of the various ways that this can be done. A major element is how, through leadership, we can help to create the right conditions and appropriate context for good practice. This is essentially about the leadership capabilities of sense-making, relating and visioning, but also influencing. As we discussed in Chapter 4, this needs to take place in many different, often overlapping, spheres, using different methods. It includes professional networks and communities of practice; partnerships with service users and carers; academia; policy-making circles; health and social care and other organisations; social media; and in wider society.

Leadership and professional socialisation

Another significant element to note is how professional leadership is not just seen as playing an important role in professional development (of self and others), but also in the process of *professional socialisation*. 'Professional socialisation' is a term often used to describe the process by which those joining and working in a profession learn the skills and knowledge, but also the attitudes, behaviour and roles appropriate to that particular profession (Miller, 2010). A key part of professional socialisation is how we develop working relationships (both formal and informal) with our fellow professionals and team members from other professions (Higgs, 2013). It has also been described as the process by which we internalise professional norms and values and develop our sense of professional identity (Chatman, 1991; Webb, 2017). So, while concepts of professional socialisation and professional development greatly overlap, there is an added dimension to professional socialisation. Over and above learning the necessary skills and values, and acquiring the necessary knowledge and keeping up to date, the process of professional socialisation includes how we learn to act like a professional, how to fit in to professional culture, take on the professional identity, to develop professional habits of mind (Epstein and Hundert, 2002) – in short, how to *be* professional in ways that are acceptable and recognisable to other professionals. Higgs (2013, p. 86) explains professional socialisation as not only the process of how newcomers to a professional role learn to 'walk the walk' and 'talk the talk', but also how they learn to 'think the think'. In even more colloquial terms, we might describe this as the process of how we 'learn the ropes'. Learning the ropes need not just apply to starting a new job or someone entering the profession. At all levels within the profession we need to 'learn the ropes' whenever we step into a new role. Professional socialisation inevitably involves formal procedures such as organisational inductions and training courses, but also informal processes such as observing and talking with others – 'learning on the job'.

Activity 5.3 Professional socialisation: 'Learning the ropes'

Discuss the following questions.

1. Think about a time when you started a new job or role. What helped you 'learn the ropes'?
2. Think about a time when you struggled to learn a new role properly. What would have helped you to learn better?
3. What do you think that 'learning the ropes' means when applied to social work? Does enabling others to practise social work professionally require professional leadership? If so, in what ways?

Commentary

Responses will vary to the first two questions. However, it is likely that in learning a new role informal methods might be valued equally if not more so than formal methods. Inductions and other formal training programmes are important, but can never quite be tailored to every individual's specific needs in terms of timing, teaching method and other factors such as our personal learning style. This highlights the important role played by our fellow workers on a day-to-day basis. Most of us value others taking the time to explain things to us. At times, this might have been especially valued when we lacked the confidence to ask. It probably helped when more experienced staff were proactive rather than reactive in offering help and guidance. Experienced staff need to look out for their experienced colleagues, using their experience to anticipate what their less experienced colleagues need to know – without waiting to be asked.

We all have different learning styles, but many people learn by observing what others do. Learning job roles can often be made easier by shadowing others or working jointly with more senior colleagues. This underlines the importance of *professional role models* in the workplace (see below). It is therefore evident that we learn new job roles through a mix of informal and formal methods. In both cases we are reliant on others not only to explain, but also to demonstrate what is expected of us professionally.

We can struggle to learn a role for a variety of reasons. These include: when job roles are vague and poorly explained; when we do not fully understand the standards expected; when examples of good practice are not available; when colleagues are busy, remote and seemingly unapproachable; when we do not receive guidance or feedback on how we are doing; and when we are left alone by others and expected to work things out on our own. Sometimes learning new roles is made more difficult when others expect too much too soon and do not make allowances for the time it takes to properly acquire new knowledge and learn new skills. All of this points to a lack of effective leadership. Therefore, most people learn better when their learning needs are taken into account; they are given clear instructions; they are properly supported and guided and provided with examples of good practice. Most people also appreciate being given the opportunity to ask questions and to seek reassurance on progress. This reflects good leadership in the workplace – and, as we have discussed throughout, it need not come solely from managers.

Social work is a complex professional activity which takes place in contexts that are ever changing. Consequently, 'learning the ropes' properly is inevitably an ongoing process. However, current regulatory guidance (for example, the PCF and KSSs) lays out what level of capability is expected at specific levels and in what areas of social work. Therefore, while no one would expect any individual to know everything there is to know about social work, there are certain standards expected depending on where we are in terms of our career and in which branch of social work we practise. It is our professional responsibility to know what these are.

It is important to stress that, at any level, 'learning the ropes' of social work is *not* simply about learning organisational procedures and systems. It is about understanding how to think critically, analyse, use evidence and make appropriate decisions under conditions of uncertainty. It is also about the ability to practise in accordance with relevant legislation, policy and, importantly, social work principles.

There are several formal leadership roles within social work devoted to ensuring that people 'learn the ropes' properly. Managers, those in workforce development, supervisors and practice educators all play a part in ensuring that the social work workforce is professionally trained and supervised. In addition, various mentoring and coaching schemes have also been introduced in different contexts with varying degrees of success (HSCB, 2014; BASW, 2015b). All of these could be said to play formal leadership roles in that it is part of the job description to facilitate others' learning, develop professional practice and ensure that practice meets the necessary professional standards. However, there are important informal leadership roles that are played in enabling someone to learn the ropes properly. If a defining characteristic of leadership is the ability to influence others to achieve common goals (Northouse, 2015a) then we need to be mindful of both the formal and informal means by which this happens.

In the next section we focus on two important activities where professional leadership takes place outside of formal job roles but, nevertheless, plays a critical part in professional socialisation. These are: role modelling and informal supervision activities (including informal mentoring and *ad hoc* case discussions).

Role modelling

The idea of role modelling links to social learning theory (Bandura, 1977). Role modelling is when the way someone behaves serves as an example of the values, attitudes and behaviours associated with a particular role. It takes place whether we are aware of it or not. The importance of role modelling in developing good practice is recognised across the caring professions (Murray and Main, 2005; Cruess, Cruess and Steinert, 2008). The leadership we demonstrate through our behaviour as role models can be positive but also negative. For example, the leader who wants his or her team to be punctual to meetings and treat each other respectfully needs to model those behaviours themselves or risk undermining their authority or credibility and subverting any messages they wish to give. When we are followers we pick up cues from those we consider leaders about what are acceptable and unacceptable ways of behaving. This happens unconsciously anyway. However, if we operate in an environment where there is critical reflection on practice, the behaviour of the role model and skills and the values therein embodied will be brought much more closely into focus.

Cruess et al. (2008) explain how role model behaviour can either be passively (unconsciously) incorporated into practice or more actively (consciously) explored for more general principles. The classic example of passive role model learning, for example, would be when young children 'naturally' and uncritically copy what their parents do without thinking about it. Active exploration of role model behaviour involves reflecting critically on what has been observed, developing insights, abstracting general principles and putting them into action. The model presented by Cruess et al. is not dissimilar to the learning cycle proposed by Kolb and Fry (1974). This highlights that we all learn something from experience, but that a better quality of learning takes place when concrete experiences are explored and reflected upon critically.

Characteristics of positive role models include that they enjoy their work; are professionally competent; and lead by example (Murray and Main, 2005). Positive professional role modelling is important for effective professional socialisation, but it is also important in order to provide a positive image of social work to service users, carers, other professionals and the outside world generally. Thus role modelling is an important leadership function *inside* and *outside* the profession.

Key points about leadership through role modelling

- Less experienced practitioners (followers) use their observations of the behaviour of more experienced practitioners (leaders) to acquire professional knowledge, skills and values and to internalise professional norms. This process can either be informal and passive/unconscious or more formal and critically reflective.

- The importance of role modelling for professional socialisation suggests that we need to practise both reflectively and reflexively (Knott and Scragg, 2016) or else run the risk of providing ineffective leadership through poor role modelling of practice.

- Role modelling underlines the importance of leader–follower relationship and the need for both self-awareness and good communication. We need to be prepared to explain our practice to others clearly and in a way that leaves space for challenge, feedback, questions and constructive criticism. Followers need to maintain a critically reflective stance on the practice they observe and to be prepared to question and challenge assertively but respectfully.

- Having clarity about competence and confidence in our role as social workers is important when acting as role model/leader for social work colleagues, but also with service users, carers and other professionals.

Supervision

Supervision and other related activities, such as mentoring and coaching, represent a very important means by which social workers learn how to be social workers (see Fenge and

Field, 2016, for a discussion of the overlaps and differences between the three activities). The need for and benefits of supervision in developing professionalism in social work has long been embedded in professional guidance (BASW, 2011; BASW, 2018b). While supervision on its own should not necessarily be regarded as professional leadership it nevertheless provides many opportunities for professional leadership. Supervision in its broadest sense can vary in its degree of formality and the extent to which it is a planned activity. Both formal and informal supervision in social work can take different forms with different purposes (Wonnacott, 2012; Fenge and Field, 2016).

Not all supervision is professional supervision

Supervisors in social work are usually both representatives of their organisation and of their profession. The extent to which they represent their profession will depend on their role and the organisational context (Bogo, 2013). We therefore need to make the distinction between managerial supervision and professional supervision. Managerial supervision tends to be directive, disciplinary and focuses more on productivity and quality assurance. This can be experienced negatively by practitioners, especially if there is no support dimension (ibid.). Professional supervision is more facilitative and focuses more on professional learning and emotional support (Fenge and Field, 2016). As current regulatory guidance regards supervision as an activity of professional leadership it is therefore assumed here that when we talk about supervision it is of the professional kind. In many social work organisations formal supervision is a hybrid in that it combines elements of both forms. However, organisations can and do deliver the two forms separately depending on the context. The distinction must be highlighted as it must not be assumed that supervision in itself provides professional leadership or that supervision is carried out by a qualified social worker. Key messages from literature reviews are that good supervision is correlated with perceived worker effectiveness (Carpenter and Webb, 2012) and that it has a 'positive effect of supervision on staff, particularly the education function' (Bogo, 2013, p. 157). It should be noted that Bogo also highlights the 'scant evidence base related to client outcome' (ibid.), which reminds us that, whatever form it takes and in whatever context, supervision needs to retain sight of a service user focus.

Formal, informal, planned and ad hoc supervision

Wonnacott (2012, p. 65) draws our attention to the fact that in social work practitioners support, mentor and supervise each other in diverse ways. These ways will vary in the extent to which they are formal or informal, planned or *ad hoc*. So, for example, the classic formal, planned supervision would be the scheduled monthly meeting between supervisor and supervisee based around a pre-planned agenda. This, argues Wonnacott, provides consistency, predictability and regularity, but she cautions that in fast-paced and changing situations this method cannot be relied upon alone. However, often formal supervision meetings are held between scheduled meetings in response to a specific issue or critical incident. While these can very useful for debriefing purposes or making urgent decisions, Wonnacott warns against relying solely on this method, arguing that, being incident specific, it is unlikely to address long-term development needs. Supervision and mentoring can also be planned but informal, such as arranging to have a discussion with the social worker after a visit on the phone or in the car, often without a set agenda. Wonnacott argues that on such occasions this type of supervision can provide support where more formal discussion is not possible, but argues that there are dangers when such discussions are not recorded. Lastly, *ad hoc* informal discussions are those such as one might have spontaneously by the water cooler or in the stairwell at work. These happen all the time in social work settings and can last as little as a few minutes or much longer. Wonnacott recognises that they have some limited value as a method of reassuring colleagues, but believes that these types of discussion might create issues such as confidentiality breaches, as well as short-cutting proper reflection, leading to flawed decision making.

Being proficient in a formal supervisory role is clearly important in order to be an effective professional leader (Davys and Beddoe, 2010; Wonnacott, 2012; Howe and Gray, 2013; Fenge and Field, 2016). However, an additional leadership challenge is to be able to assess when a degree of supervisory intervention is needed informally and then deliver it in the most appropriate way. Supervision need not wait until the next planned session, nor should it not take place because someone's 'official' supervisor is not available. An *ad hoc* conversation offered at the right time could be both supportive and transformational in a colleague's practice. This is an example of situational leadership. Often colleagues do not ask for help for a variety of reasons, but need it nevertheless, suggesting that we need to think about the particular leadership skills required in such circumstances.

A great deal of literature on the subject focuses on supervision and mentoring as formal, planned activities (Carpenter and Webb, 2012; HSCB, 2014). However, the informal and *ad hoc* supervision, mentoring and coaching that take place can often be overlooked as an important opportunity for professional leadership. It is therefore to this area that we give our attention, although there are, of course, many overlaps.

Skills of supervision in relation to leadership

The essential skills and qualities required by professional supervisors and professional leaders are the same. In fact, they are the capabilities of professional social work generally. They include: competence as a practitioner; sensitivity to wider contextual issues; communication and interpersonal skills; emotional intelligence and empathy (see below); the ability to build and manage relationships; the ability to manage power and authority; critical thinking and questioning and giving and receiving feedback (Davys and Beddoe, 2010; Howe and Gray, 2013;

Kadushin and Harkins, 2003). However, as discussed, the idea of leadership implies use of initiative and the ability to be proactive. Therefore, to be effective we need to have our 'antennae' out for the learning needs of others when the occasion requires it and not just wait for planned supervision sessions. Here emotional intelligence and empathy are important qualities to possess.

The importance of emotional intelligence and empathy in helping others develop their practice

If we are going to be appropriately proactive and responsive in enabling others to learn as professionals, then we need to possess both emotional intelligence and empathy (Wonnacott, 2012; Ingram, 2013; McKitterick, 2015; Fairtlough, 2017). In the context of leadership Fairtlough (2017, p. 88) has highlighted the importance of 'eliciting skills', among which 'empathic divining' plays an important part. Therefore, to demonstrate professional leadership in enabling others to learn, we need to be able to pick up on and identify emotions in ourselves and others. (Refer back to Chapter 3 for more on the relationship between leadership and emotional intelligence.) Professional leadership in social work means recognising the important part that emotions play in all aspects of social work practice, and that includes decision-making and learning (Howe, 2008; Ingram, 2013). We will be more effective in a leadership role if we can read the emotional temperature of those around us, understand their needs better and take anticipatory action. This is something that is more likely to happen effectively if we work in an organisational environment that values and fosters relationship building and provides 'safe spaces' where practitioners can talk about their feelings and where they can express self-doubt about competence without being judged negatively (Parker and Doel, 2013).

Empathy means being able to see the world through the other person's eyes. We need to be able to recognise where colleagues might be out of their depth or struggling to practise

Activity 5.4 Practising leadership through *ad hoc* and informal supervision

- Reflect upon a situation where you took the lead and offered *ad hoc* or informal supervision to a colleague. What prompted you to intervene? What form did it take? Was it effective? If not, give reasons.
- Reflect upon a situation where you could have offered *ad hoc* or informal supervision but did not for some reason. Why did you not intervene? What might you have done differently?

professionally due to inexperience or lack of knowledge. Leadership comes in when the appropriate advice, support or learning is offered when it is needed.

Commentary

Spotting when someone is need of advice or support is not always straightforward. If we are busy or distracted then we will not be attentive to the needs of others and pick up the necessary cues. Also, sometimes the cues are not obvious. For example, just because someone is sitting quietly at their desk studying their computer does not mean that they are not struggling to know how to deal with a situation. This underlines not only the importance of empathy and emotional intelligence, but also a proactive mindset that anticipates people's potential needs and sees the value of activities such as checking in with people – especially when we know that someone is new or that they are dealing with a new situation. People do not always ask for help for a variety of reasons – often it is anxiety about appearing incompetent. This highlights that is often *how* support is offered that is critical. For example, if it is offered in a way that reinforces feelings of inadequacy – for example, in public with a tone of exasperation – then that person will probably never ask for help again and neither will anyone else in the office.

There are various reasons why we might not offer supervisory assistance to a colleague who needs it. It could be that we are not aware of their need in the first place, or it might be that we lack the time, that our energies are depleted through stress or we feel that it is not our place as, for example, there may be an official mentoring system already in place. Failure to demonstrate leadership in this way is not necessarily a personal failing; it is as much a symptom of a dysfunctional organisational culture. *Ad hoc* and informal supervision is more likely to take place and is more likely to be effective if the overall organisational and team environment is facilitative, mutually supporting, is committed to social work principles and where this form of professional leadership is modelled positively. However, in Chapter 4 we reviewed factors that hinder professional leadership taking place. Therefore, given that organisational contexts may not support what we might think of as exemplary forms of supervision at all times, we can fall back on the logic presented by collective and situational leadership. That is to say, all of us need to offer what we are good at, when the situation needs it.

These final two sections have focused on the importance of role modelling, supervision and mentoring in professional leadership in social work. However, it is recommended that readers should check out the most recent versions of the PCF and other professional guidance for what is stated about professional leadership. As has been pointed out on numerous occasions throughout the book, in social work, ideas change and so does the guidance to social workers. This reflects both the influence of professional leadership in producing these changes and the need for further professional leadership in interpreting them and putting them into practice.

Chapter summary

- Broadly, professional leadership involves the capabilities of sense-making; relating; visioning; and inventing. To this we can add the ability to influence others to achieve a common goal. No single person can expect to be fully competent in all these areas at all times.
- Professional leadership in social work utilises the same skills, qualities and knowledge as are required in most social work practice. However, to be effective professional leadership requires high levels of skills in communication, relationship building and critical reflection. You need to be able to influence and motivate others.
- Professional leadership also requires a certain professional mindset. This mindset includes curiosity about matters that affect social work, together with the ability to use initiative and imagination, to be proactive and to be innovative.
- Tenacity, commitment and passion are also important leadership qualities.
- We need to remember the importance of the leader–follower relationship. Therefore, as well as ensuring that we have the skills and qualities to take the lead when necessary, we also need to ensure that we have the skills and qualities to be effective followers. We need to be able to enable leadership in others when the situation requires it.
- Current guidance on professional leadership emphasises that we develop and show leadership, individually and collectively, through promoting social work's purpose, practice and impact; we promote organisational contexts conducive to good practice and learning; we work in partnership with people who use services and stakeholders to develop our leadership and aims for the profession.
- Positive role modelling and offering colleagues supervision and mentoring are both effective ways of providing professional leadership in everyday situations.

Further reading

Fairtlough, A (2017) *Professional leadership for social workers and educators*. London: Routledge.

This is a very good text that discusses leadership theory and provides many relevant examples of how professional leadership can be put into practice in social work.

Field, R and Brown, K (2016) (2nd edn) *Effective leadership, management and supervision in health and social care*. Exeter: Learning Matters.

Although primarily aimed at managers and senior practitioners, this text contains very useful chapters on topics such as 'Self-leadership' and 'Supervision'.

McKitterick, B (2015) *Self-leadership in social work: Reflections from practice*. Bristol: Policy Press.

Although its focus is 'self-leadership', this text contains many ideas and examples that are relevant to professional leadership in social work generally.

Shearer, J (2018) Social work leaders must stop hiding and give our profession a voice, *The Guardian Social Care Network*. Online at: https://www.theguardian.com/social-care-network/social-life-blog/2018/jan/16/social-work-leaders-must-stop-hiding-and-give-our-profession-a-voice

This article is a good example of professional leadership in itself; it makes the case for better leadership not only at the top, but also throughout the social work profession.

Templeton, R (2016) Improving social work relies on innovative practitioners and service users, not big ideas. *Community Care*, 20 January. Available online at: http://www.communitycare.co.uk/2016/01/20/improving-social-work-relies-practitioners-service-users-big-ideas/

A good article that argues that being innovative is something any social worker can and should do if services are to improve.

6: Preparing for Professional Leadership Challenges Ahead

Achieving a social work degree

This chapter will enable you to develop the following capabilities to the appropriate level from the PCF:

- critical reflection and analysis
- intervention and skills
- contexts and organisations
- professional leadership
- professionalism.

It will also introduce you to the following academic standards as set out in the social work subject benchmark statement:

5.2 Social Work theory
5.3 Values and ethics
5.4 Service users and carers
5.5 The nature of Social Work practice, in the UK and more widely
5.6 The leadership, organisation and delivery of Social Work services
5.10 Problem-solving skills
5.15 Communication skills
5.16 Skills in working with others
5.17 Skills in personal and professional development

More specifically it will enable you to:

- reflect upon and prepare for the professional leadership challenges facing social work now and in the future;
- consider a range of specific ways in which professional leadership can be demonstrated in different practice settings at the student social worker, newly qualified and social worker level.

Introduction

As explained at the beginning, this is a book on leadership aimed primarily at social work students and newly qualified social workers and not managers or others who hold formal leadership roles in organisations. We have explained that while there are overlaps between leadership and management they are not the same thing. Professional leadership in social work is something we all need to take responsibility for. In this context we have seen that leadership can mean many things, but most would agree that a key ingredient involves being active and proactive rather than passive and reactive. Basic elements in leadership are the ability to take responsibility, think for ourselves and to use our initiative. We have stressed the importance of both sense-making and visioning as core leadership capabilities. We have also highlighted the skills of being able to communicate effectively with, relate to and influence others. We, therefore, begin by revisiting key issues raised in previous chapters which we all must try to make sense of and do something about if social work is to progress as a professional occupation. The first activity aims to stimulate your thinking on some of the 'big' questions of social work, all of which encompass or touch on ideas about professionalism, social work and leadership. You are encouraged to think about how and where you might make a leadership contribution.

While the first part of the chapter is concerned with the bigger leadership challenges facing social work generally, the second part focuses on actual day-to-day micro-leadership activities that can be undertaken in particular settings. What links the two parts is that any leadership activity needs to be informed by our sense of what the bigger picture is and also by how we believe professional social work should be practised. Practical suggestions for how collective and situational leadership might be demonstrated at student social worker, newly qualified social worker and social worker levels are offered. They are not proposed to be carried out unthinkingly, simply to tick the 'leadership' box. For us to genuinely say we have practised leadership we must have our own reasons about why we want to undertake an activity. The impetus to action must come from us to some degree. The chapter concludes with suggestions for further reading and further development activities.

Activity 6.1 Questions for professional social work

The following questions track key themes and issues discussed in previous chapters. They concern social work generally and are not exhaustive of all the specific micro-challenges facing social work in its different settings. However, many of the questions could equally be directed at specific services. It would be useful to exchange views with a partner or in a small group as you should be able to explain, evidence or justify your responses.

1. Is the professionalisation of social work a good thing for a) social workers and b) service users? Explain your answer.
2. What should be the defining characteristics of social work as a profession?
3. What, if anything is to be learned from social work's past that would help it develop in the future?
4. Explain where you think social work is going as a profession. Also, what do you think are the drivers for change and are you happy with the direction social work is going? Give reasons.
5. In what ways would *you* like to see professional social work change? Explain your answer.
6. What are the biggest challenges facing social work? What needs to happen in order to respond effectively and what are the criteria for success?
7. How does the leadership of social work need to develop to make it more effective in meeting the challenges facing the profession?
8. How can we be better prepared for leadership roles in social work?
9. What are you able to do in terms of developing the professional leadership of social work? What are your leadership strengths?
10. How can you enable others to be better professionals and to be more effective social workers?

Lastly

11. How can you better prepare to respond to these questions?

Commentary

From 1 to 10 they are, in the main, large, complex questions. The debates are ongoing. There are no simple answers and neither is there a set formula for how to respond. However, in respect of question 11, to provide responses that are both credible and justifiable you need to have a genuine interest in social work, coupled with the ability to think analytically. It would help if you maintained an open mind, kept up to date, read widely and considered different perspectives, not just on social work, but also on the many factors that impact on social work.

Context is all

Among other things, we have seen how professional guidance expects social workers to practise leadership to 'promote organisational contexts conducive to good practice and learning' (BASW, 2018b). We therefore need to understand the many and various contexts in which diverse social work organisations operate. Consequently, it would help if you had a reasonable sense of social work's history and of the current global, political and economic context in which it currently takes place (Pierson, 2011). Perhaps more importantly, to be able to fully understand and practise social work, you need to be able to understand it in both its social and sociological context (Ingleby, 2018). A key part of this is understanding the policy and legislative context – but also the driving forces behind any policies and legislation (Thompson, 2015). In this respect, being politically aware, being part of networks and associations, attending conferences and workshops and following relevant individuals and groups online would all be helpful activities.

Leadership activities

Activity 6.1 was primarily focused on the larger questions of social work. It is for the profession as a whole to engage with these and other big questions, not just a few individuals in senior positions. We can all make a contribution collectively by thinking critically, contributing to debates, having conversations and sharing our views formally and informally in appropriate fora and through appropriate channels. However, leadership isn't just about engaging with the 'big' macro questions, important as they are. As individuals we can demonstrate professional leadership more tangibly and on a smaller micro scale in a variety of ways in our day-to-day practice when the situation demands it. The activities listed below are suggestions for how professional leadership might be demonstrated at different levels. They cover a variety of leadership roles and functions but do not claim to be comprehensive by any means. The important *caveat* is that just doing them because they are on the list does not demonstrate leadership. They can only be said to be examples of leadership if they are genuinely inspired by a desire to make a positive difference to social work in some way. The impetus to do something must originate with you.

Student social worker

At the student social worker level, as we feel ourselves into the role (learn the ropes), mostly our activities are likely to come under the heading of active followership. However, there will always be leadership opportunities, and active followership in the first placement can often form the bridge to actual leadership in the second. Ideas and opportunities for leadership will emerge from critical reflection and a preparedness to use initiative and take responsibility when the situation requires it.

In the classroom/university

- Ask questions, seek clarification of key concepts and theories (remember, also, the importance of individual and collective sense-making to leadership). Think about the case of Chloe discussed in the Introduction.

- Provide constructive feedback in response to answers given.

- Enable others to improve the quality of their work.

- Actively engage in debates and discussions on social work and also on social and political issues and current affairs. Make sure that you and others are up to date by making relevant contributions in class.

- Keep abreast of and contribute to social work discussions online. Follow Chief Social Workers, social work organisations and social work academics on Twitter and other social media – think critically about what you read. Share relevant content.

- Share interesting and relevant journal articles.

- Initiate and/or contribute to support or study groups.

- Organise talks by internal and external speakers. These do not have to be professionals; much can be gained from inviting in service users and carers. Remember to be professional and welcoming whenever you undertake this type of activity.

- Network, join and contribute to relevant local, regional and national social work organisations. Make links with local service user groups or other relevant organisations. Disseminate information to your peers and lecturers.

- Be a student ambassador at open days and other social work marketing and recruitment events.

- Become a student representative for your class or faculty as part of your university's system of participation.

- Help to improve the learning experience for everyone by reaching out to isolated individuals and groups. Work to combat oppressive behaviour such as malicious gossiping and group in-fighting. Help make the classroom/university a safe and supportive space for learning and exchange of views.

- Organise and participate in peer support and mentoring.

- Organise and participate in activities that improve group morale and group cohesion.

- Role model professional behaviour both inside and outside the university.

Suggested leadership activities for students on first placement

In the first placement genuine opportunities for leadership might be limited. However, remember that collective leadership requires different roles to be played and also do not forget the importance of being an active follower when others are leading. The activities are about developing a leadership mindset; that is to say, they require you to be 'switched on', think about what it is to be professional, to take the initiative at appropriate times and to enable the learning of others where possible. Clearly, you need not undertake all of them. In your first placement one example of genuine leadership would be sufficient.

- Observe and reflect critically upon the professionalism (and professional leadership) of those whom you work with. Share your views with others, including your practice educator and on-site supervisor.

- Be prepared to share learning from university with the team where appropriate.

- During any induction visits, collect information for dissemination with others; also provide a positive role model for social work by being punctual, respectful, attentive and so on.

- Contribute to development in your organisation/agency that improves the way it promotes social work values.

- Make a relevant contribution to a group discussion or a short presentation in a meeting that promotes critical thinking about an aspect of social work.

- Observe and critically reflect upon professionals undertaking action in different settings – for example, in meetings, around the office, in court, home visits and interviewing. If you have the opportunity discuss with them afterwards what they thought was professional about their practice.

- Observe and critically reflect upon how a professional practitioner leads/chairs formal meetings that include service users and those that do not. If you have the opportunity, discuss with them afterwards what they thought was professional about their practice.

- Report back to other team members the content and learning of any training undertaken.

- Research a topic of relevance to share with the team. A good topic could be seeking the views of service users about the service.

- Contact those in professional leadership positions – for example, principal social workers – and ask them about their role. How do they conceive of professional leadership in their role and the roles of others such as student social workers and newly qualified social workers?

- Think of ways in which the organisation/team can actively encourage meaningful service user participation. If it does already, as many teams will do, think about how this can be improved and/or disseminated.

Additional leadership activities suggested for students on final placement

Most of the activities suggested above would be equally applicable in a final placement. However, with more experience and knowledge you should be more confident. You should expect to take more responsibility, be more proactive and be more prepared to use your initiative and step up to:

- identify and then attend an appropriate training event and disseminate/cascade knowledge;

- brief and guide (be a mentor to) first placement students;

- chair (or take minutes of) an appropriate meeting;

- help organise and participate in peer supervision/action learning sets;

- organise an appropriate training event for colleagues/service users/carers;

- conduct evaluation or focus group research with service users/carers;

- run a group/workshop for service users/carers;

- take a lead role in a piece of work, particularly where it involves liaison with other agencies;

- on completion, present a reflective report back to the team/team manager, offering opinions of strengths and weaknesses;

- join national social work organisations as a student member.

Practice placements require you to reflect critically on and learn from your experiences across all the domains. However, if you undertake any of the activities suggested above, you will develop your leadership capabilities by focusing your reflections on certain points, including:

- Explain how you demonstrated leadership.

- What was the rationale for doing what you did in terms of your own professional development and that of others?

- How did you influence others?

- What impact did you make on the service?

- What did you do well and in what ways could you have improved? Give reasons.

Leadership opportunities suggested for newly qualified social workers

> *While an NQSW may feel a 'rookie', they are often the best placed to introduce a critical awareness and new thinking in practice and public policy research.*

> McKitterick, 2015, p. 123

McKitterick makes a very good point. Even though it might not feel like it, in many ways newly qualified social workers are in an ideal position to make leadership contributions. Having just qualified, you will have a strong sense of social work issues, social work theories, social work values and will have habituated sound professional practices such as critical reflection. Importantly, you will not have settled into familiar, uncritical and institutionalised ways of thinking and practising, which can sometimes mean that sub-optimal standards of practice become normalised and taken for granted. This can happen with any practitioner who has been in the job for a while. As McKitterick suggests, use this opportunity to share your observations constructively in order to stimulate reflection and debate within the team. Making sure that you do not cross the boundaries of confidentiality, share your reflections in professional networks.

In terms of actual leadership activities, many of those suggested for student social workers are applicable. However, it is to be expected that as you gather more experience and develop your knowledge and skills, the degree of responsibility and initiative demonstrated should increase accordingly. To the leadership activities already suggested the following could be added:

- supervision – in varying degrees of formality and in different forms;
- coaching and mentoring students and peers (Fenge and Field, 2016);
- full engagement in the life of the team and wider community – for example, representing the team in local and regional groups;
- networking with other NQSWs;
- joining and taking an active part in national social work organisations/unions;
- creative identification of your own learning needs and ongoing continuing professional development (CPD), with the appropriate cascade of learning to colleagues, during and/or afterwards.

Leadership opportunities for social workers

By this stage your professional leadership mindset and leadership capabilities should have developed to the point where you have your own ideas for leadership activities. However, one point to note is that professional guidance indicates that the more experienced we are, the more responsibility we need to take in contributing to both the development of the service and the learning of others (BASW, 2018b). Social workers should therefore be thinking about taking on practice leader/supervisor responsibilities (Department for Education, 2015) and obtaining Stage 1 and Stage 2 of the *Practice educator professional standards* (PEPS) (TCSW/BASW, 2012).

Also by the social worker level you should definitely be thinking in terms of professional leadership not only within your own organisation, but also *across* organisations (Fairtlough, 2017). This can be through contributing towards inter-agency learning, but also by representing the social work perspective in multi-disciplinary settings of various kinds and also service user groups. Both social workers and newly qualified social workers should actively engage with any governmental consultation exercises where a social work perspective is required. When individual views are expressed – as opposed to through a professional body – they can be critical but they must be constructive, professionally expressed and in line with social work ethics and values, otherwise you might inadvertently cause a degree of reputational damage for your organisation and/or for social work generally.

Chapter summary

This chapter has been relatively short. However, it was primarily designed to remind you of the three important interconnected themes of the first three chapters of the book, which are that:

1. How you think about professionalism and what you think is 'professional' will strongly influence how you practise as a professional.
2. How you think about social work and what its function is in society will strongly influence how you practice social work – and perhaps most importantly given the focus of this book.
3. How you think about leadership will strongly influence how you practice leadership.

None of these questions is ever settled. Nevertheless, to be able to practise professional leadership in social work effectively you must engage seriously with these and other big conceptual questions.

Because of the large and complex nature of the questions, the latter chapters of the book were designed with the purpose of giving you some concrete and tangible suggestions to think about and to try out in practice, all the while remembering that genuine leadership requires you to see the opportunity and take appropriate action.

Further reading

Davies, K and Ross, J (2016) Skills for leadership, in Davies, K and Jones, R (eds) *Skills for social work practice.* Basingstoke: Palgrave: 162–77.

This chapter is good on skills development, but also makes useful suggestions about leadership opportunities at the pre- and post-registration level.

Fairtlough, A (2017) *Professional leadership for social workers and educators*. London: Routledge.

This is a very good text that discusses leadership theory and provides many relevant examples of how professional leadership can be put into practice in social work.

Ingleby, E (2018) *Applied sociology for social work*. London: Sage.

This is a very useful introduction to sociological concepts and theories and how they might be applied to social work in ways which improve practice.

McKitterick, B (2015) *Self-leadership in social work: Reflections from practice*. Bristol: Policy Press.

Although its focus is 'self-leadership', this text contains many ideas and examples that are relevant to professional leadership in social work generally.

Appendix 1

Professional Capabilities Framework (2018)

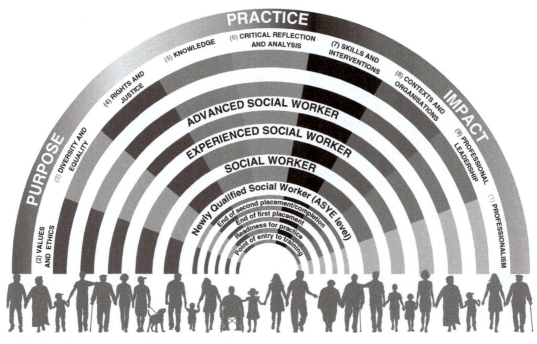

Published with kind permission of BASW – www.basw.co.uk

Appendix 2

Subject Benchmark for Social Work

5 Knowledge, understanding and skills

Subject knowledge and understanding

5.1 During their qualifying degree studies in Social Work, students acquire, critically evaluate, apply and integrate knowledge and understanding in the following five core areas of study.

5.2 Social Work theory, which includes:

  i   critical explanations from Social Work theory and other subjects which contribute to the knowledge base of Social Work

 ii   an understanding of Social Work's rich and contested history from both a UK and comparative perspective

iii   the relevance of sociological and applied psychological perspectives to understanding societal and structural influences on human behaviour at individual, group and community levels, and the relevance of sociological theorisation to a deeper understanding of adaptation and change

 iv   the relevance of psychological, physical and physiological perspectives to understanding human, personal and social development, well-being and risk

  v   social science theories explaining and exploring group and organisational behaviour

 vi   the range of theories and research informed evidence that informs understanding of the child, adult, family or community and of the range of assessment and interventions which can be used

vii   the theory, models and methods of assessment, factors underpinning the selection and testing of relevant information, knowledge and critical appraisal of relevant social science and other research and evaluation methodologies, and the evidence base for Social Work

viii   the nature of analysis and professional judgement and the processes of risk assessment and decision making, including the theory of risk informed decisions and the balance of choice and control, rights and protection in decision making

 ix   approaches, methods and theories of intervention in working with a diverse population within a wide range of settings, including factors.

5.3 Values and ethics, which include:

i   the nature, historical evolution, political context and application of professional Social Work values, informed by national and international definitions and ethical statements, and their relation to personal values, identities, influences and ideologies

ii   the ethical concepts of rights, responsibility, freedom, authority and power inherent in the practice of social workers as agents with statutory powers in different situations

iii   aspects of philosophical ethics relevant to the understanding and resolution of value dilemmas and conflicts in both interpersonal and professional contexts

iv   understanding of, and adherence to, the ethical foundations of empirical and conceptual research, as both consumers and producers of social science research

v   the relationship between human rights enshrined in law and the moral and ethical rights determined theoretically, philosophically and by contemporary society

vi   the complex relationships between justice, care and control in social welfare and the practical and ethical implications of these, including their expression in roles as statutory agents in diverse practice settings and in upholding the law in respect of challenging discrimination and inequalities

vii   the conceptual links between codes defining ethical practice and the regulation of professional conduct

viii   the professional and ethical management of potential conflicts generated by codes of practice held by different professional groups

ix   the ethical management of professional dilemmas and conflicts in balancing the perspectives of individuals who need care and support and professional decision making at points of risk, care and protection

x   the constructive challenging of individuals and organisations where there may be conflicts with Social Work values, ethics and codes of practice

xi   the professional responsibility to be open and honest if things go wrong (the duty of candour about own practice) and to act on concerns about poor or unlawful practice by any person or organisation

xii   continuous professional development as a reflective, informed and skilled practitioner, including the constructive use of professional supervision.

5.4 Service users and carers, which include:

i   the factors which contribute to the health and well-being of individuals, families and communities, including promoting dignity, choice and independence for people who need care and support

   ii   the underpinning perspectives that determine explanations of the characteristics and circumstances of people who need care and support, with critical evaluation drawing on research, practice experience and the experience and expertise of people who use services

   iii   the social and psychological processes associated with, for example, poverty, migration, unemployment, trauma, poor health, disability, lack of education and other sources of disadvantage and how they affect well-being, how they interact and may lead to marginalisation, isolation and exclusion, and demand for Social Work services

   iv   explanations of the links between the factors contributing to social differences and identities (for example, social class, gender, ethnic differences, age, sexuality and religious belief) and the structural consequences of inequality and differential need faced by service users

   v   the nature and function of Social Work in a diverse and increasingly global society (with particular reference to prejudice, interpersonal relations, discrimination, empowerment and anti-discriminatory practices).

5.5 The nature of Social Work practice, in the UK and more widely, which includes:

   i   the place of theoretical perspectives and evidence from European and international research in assessment and decision-making processes

   ii   the integration of theoretical perspectives and evidence from European and international research into the design and implementation of effective Social Work intervention with a wide range of service users, carers and communities

   iii   the knowledge and skills which underpin effective practice, with a range of service users and in a variety of settings

   iv   the processes that facilitate and support service user and citizen rights, choice, co-production, self-governance, well-being and independence

   v   the importance of interventions that promote social justice, human rights, social cohesion, collective responsibility and respect for diversity and tackle inequalities

   vi   its delivery in a range of community-based and organisational settings spanning the statutory, voluntary and private sectors, and the changing nature of these service contexts

   vii   the factors and processes that facilitate effective interdisciplinary, interprofessional and interagency collaboration and partnership across a plurality of settings and disciplines

   viii   the importance of Social Work's contribution to intervention across service user groups, settings and levels in terms of the profession's focus on social justice, human rights, social cohesion, collective responsibility and respect for diversities

   ix   the processes of reflection and reflexivity as well as approaches for evaluating service and welfare outcomes for vulnerable people.

5.6 The leadership, organisation and delivery of Social Work services, which includes:

i   the location of contemporary Social Work within historical, comparative and global perspectives, including in the devolved nations of the UK and wider European and international contexts

ii   how the service delivery context is portrayed to service users, carers, families and communities

iii   the changing demography and cultures of communities, including European and international contexts, in which social workers practise

iv   the complex relationships between public, private, social and political philosophies, policies and priorities and the organisation and practice of Social Work, including the contested nature of these

v   the issues and trends in modern public and social policy and their relationship to contemporary practice, service delivery and leadership in Social Work

vi   the significance of legislative and legal frameworks and service delivery standards, including on core Social Work values and ethics in the delivery of services which support, enable and empower

vii   the current range and appropriateness of statutory, voluntary and private agencies providing services and the organisational systems inherent within these

viii   development of new ways of working and delivery, for example the development of social enterprises, integrated multi-professional teams and independent Social Work provision

ix   the significance of professional and organisational relationships with other related services, including housing, health, education, police, employment, fire, income maintenance and criminal justice

x   the importance and complexities of the way agencies work together to provide care, the relationships between agency policies, legal requirements and professional boundaries in shaping the nature of services provided in integrated and interdisciplinary contexts

xi   the contribution of different approaches to management and leadership within different settings, and the impact on professional practice and on quality of care management and leadership in public and human services

xii   the development of person-centred services, personalised care, individual budgets and direct payments all focusing upon the human and legal rights of the service user for control, power and self determination

xiii   the implications of modern information and communications technology for both the provision and receipt of services, use of technologically enabled support and the use of social media as a process and forum for vulnerable people, families and communities, and communities of professional practice.

Subject-specific skills and other skills

5.7 The range of skills required by a qualified social worker reflects the complex and demanding context in which they work. Many of these skills may be of value in many situations, for example, analytical thinking, building relationships, working as a member of an organisation, intervention, evaluation, and reflection. What defines the specific nature of these skills as developed by Social Work students is:

   i   the context in which they are applied and assessed (for example communication skills in practice with people with sensory impairments or assessment skills in an interprofessional setting)

   ii the relative weighting given to such skills within Social Work practice (for example the central importance of problem-solving skills within complex human situations)

   iii the specific purpose of skill development (for example the acquisition of research skills in order to build a repertoire of research-based practice)

   iv a requirement to integrate a range of skills (that is, not simply to demonstrate these in an isolated and incremental manner).

5.8 All Social Work graduates demonstrate the ability to reflect on and learn from the exercise of their skills, in order to build their professional identity. They understand the significance of the concepts of continuing professional development and lifelong learning, and accept responsibility for their own continuing development.

5.9 Social Work students acquire and integrate skills in the following five core areas.

Problem-solving skills

5.10 These are sub-divided into four areas.

5.11 Managing problem-solving activities: graduates in Social Work are able to:

   i   think logically, systematically, creatively, critically and reflectively, in order to carry out a holistic assessment

   ii apply ethical principles and practices critically in planning problem-solving activities

   iii plan a sequence of actions to achieve specified objectives, making use of research, theory and other forms of evidence

   iv manage processes of change, drawing on research, theory and other forms of evidence.

5.12 Gathering information: graduates in Social Work are able to:

    i   demonstrate persistence in gathering information from a wide range of sources and using a variety of methods, for a range of purposes. These methods include electronic searches, reviews of relevant literature, policy and procedures, face-to-face interviews, and written and telephone contact with individuals and groups

    ii   take into account differences of viewpoint in gathering information and critically assess the reliability and relevance of the information gathered

   iii   assimilate and disseminate relevant information in reports and case records.

5.13 Analysis and synthesis: graduates in Social Work are able to analyse and synthesise knowledge gathered for problem-solving purposes, in order to:

    i   assess human situations, taking into account a variety of factors (including the views of participants, theoretical concepts, research evidence, legislation and organisational policies and procedures)

    ii   analyse and synthesise information gathered, weighing competing evidence and modifying their viewpoint in the light of new information, then relate this information to a particular task, situation or problem

   iii   balance specific factors relevant to Social Work practice (such as risk, rights, cultural differences and language needs and preferences, responsibilities to protect vulnerable individuals and legal obligations)

   iv   assess the merits of contrasting theories, explanations, research, policies and procedures and use the information to develop and sustain reasoned arguments

    v   employ a critical understanding of factors that support or inhibit problem solving including societal, organisational and community issues as well as individual relationships

   vi   critically analyse and take account of the impact of inequality and discrimination in working with people who use Social Work services.

5.14 Intervention and evaluation: graduates in Social Work are able to use their knowledge of a range of interventions and evaluation processes creatively and selectively to:

    i   build and sustain purposeful relationships with people and organisations in communities and interprofessional contexts

    ii   make decisions based on evidence, set goals and construct specific plans to achieve outcomes, taking into account relevant information including ethical guidelines iii negotiate goals and plans with others, analysing and addressing in a creative and flexible manner individual, cultural and structural impediments to change

iv implement plans through a variety of systematic processes that include working in partnership

v practice in a manner that promotes well-being, protects safety and resolves conflict

vi act as a navigator, advocate and support to assist people who need care and support to take decisions and access services

vii manage the complex dynamics of dependency and, in some settings, provide direct care and personal support to assist people in their everyday lives

viii meet deadlines and comply with external requirements of a task

ix plan, implement and critically monitor and review processes and outcomes

x bring work to an effective conclusion, taking into account the implications for all involved

xi use and evaluate methods of intervention critically and reflectively.

Communication skills

5.15 Graduates in Social Work are able to communicate clearly, sensitively and effectively (using appropriate methods which may include working with interpreters) with individuals and groups of different ages and abilities in a range of formal and informal situations, in order to:

i engage individuals and organisations, who may be unwilling, by verbal, paper-based and electronic means to achieve a range of objectives, including changing behaviour

ii use verbal and non-verbal cues to guide and inform conversations and interpretation of information

iii negotiate and where necessary redefine the purpose of interactions with individuals and organisations and the boundaries of their involvement

iv listen actively and empathetically to others, taking into account their specific needs and life experiences

v engage appropriately with the life experiences of service users, to understand accurately their viewpoint, overcome personal prejudices and respond appropriately to a range of complex personal and interpersonal situations

vi make evidence informed arguments drawing from theory, research and practice wisdom including the viewpoints of service users and/or others

   vii write accurately and clearly in styles adapted to the audience, purpose and context of the communication

  viii use advocacy skills to promote others' rights, interests and needs

    ix present conclusions verbally and on paper, in a structured form, appropriate to the audience for which these have been prepared

     x make effective preparation for, and lead, meetings in a productive way.

Skills in working with others

5.16 Graduates in Social Work are able to build relationships and work effectively with others, in order to:

     i involve users of Social Work services in ways that increase their resources, capacity and power to influence factors affecting their lives

    ii engage service users and carers and wider community networks in active consultation

   iii respect and manage differences such as organisational and professional boundaries and differences of identity and/or language

   iv develop effective helping relationships and partnerships that facilitate change for individuals, groups and organisations while maintaining appropriate personal and professional boundaries

    v demonstrate interpersonal skills and emotional intelligence that creates and develops relationships based on openness, transparency and empathy

   vi increase social justice by identifying and responding to prejudice, institutional discrimination and structural inequality

   vii operate within a framework of multiple accountability (for example, to agencies, the public, service users, carers and others)

  viii observe the limits of professional and organisational responsibility, using supervision appropriately and referring to others when required

   ix provide reasoned, informed arguments to challenge others as necessary, in ways that are most likely to produce positive outcomes.

Skills in personal and professional development

5.17 Graduates in Social Work are able to:

     i work at all times in accordance with codes of professional conduct and ethics

    ii advance their own learning and understanding with a degree of independence and use supervision as a tool to aid professional development iii develop their professional identity, recognise their own professional limitations and accountability, and know how and when to seek advice from a range of sources including professional supervision

iv use support networks and professional supervision to manage uncertainty, change and stress in work situations while maintaining resilience in self and others

v handle conflict between others and internally when personal views may conflict with a course of action necessitated by the Social Work role

vi provide reasoned, informed arguments to challenge unacceptable practices in a responsible manner and raise concerns about wrongdoing in the workplace

vii be open and honest with people if things go wrong

viii understand the difference between theory, research, evidence and expertise and the role of professional judgement.

Use of technology and numerical skills

5.18 Graduates in Social Work are able to use information and communication technology effectively and appropriately for:

i professional communication, data storage and retrieval and information searching

ii accessing and assimilating information to inform working with people who use services

iii data analysis to enable effective use of research in practice

iv enhancing skills in problem-solving

v applying numerical skills to financial and budgetary responsibilities

vi understanding the social impact of technology, including the constraints of confidentiality and an awareness of the impact of the 'digital divide'.

References

Abbott, A (1988) *The system of professions: An essay on the division of expert labour*. Chicago: University of Chicago Press.

Adair, J (2009a) *Effective leadership: How to be a successful leader*. Basingstoke: Pan Macmillan.

Adair, J (2009b) *Not bosses but leaders* (3rd edn). London: Kogan Page.

Adams, R, Dominelli, L and Payne, M (2009) *Critical practice in social work*. Basingstoke: Palgrave.

Ancona, D (2005) Leadership in an age of uncertainty. Centre for eBusiness Research brief, Volume VI, 1 January.

Ancona, D, Malone, T, Orlikowski, W and Senge, P (2007) In praise of the incomplete leader. *Harvard Business Review* 85(2): 92–100.

Argyris, C (1976) Single-loop and double-loop models in research on decision making. *Administrative Science Quarterly*. 21(3): 363–75.

Argyris, C, and Schön, D (1978) *Organizational learning: A theory of action perspective*. Reading, MA: Addison-Wesley.

Ayers, S (2017) Sharing mistakes in social work means you risk being blamed and shamed. *Community Care*. Available online at: http://www.communitycare.co.uk/2017/01/25/sharing-mistakes-in-social-work-means-you-risk-being-blamed-disciplined-and-struck-off/

Backwith, D (2015) *Social work, poverty and social exclusion*. Maidenhead: Open University Press.

Bamford, T (2015) *Contemporary history of social work: Learning from the past*. Bristol: Policy Press.

Bandura, A (1977) *Social learning theory*. Englewood Cliffs, NJ: Prentice Hall.

Barclay Report (1982) *Social workers: Their roles and tasks*. London: National Institute for Social Work/Bedford Square Press.

Barrow, M (2017) When did it all go wrong between social work and the media? JKP Blog, Jessica Kingsley. Available online at: http://www.jkp.com/jkpblog/2017/03/social-work-media/

BASW (1980) *Clients are fellow citizens: Report of the working party on client participation in social work*. Birmingham: BASW.

BASW (2011) *UK supervision policy*. Available online at: http://cdn.basw.co.uk/upload/basw_73346-6.pdf

BASW (2015a) PSW magazine survey highlights poor working conditions for social workers. Available online at https://www.basw.co.uk/news/article/?id=1094

BASW (2015b) Guidelines for mentors in BASW. Available online at: https://www.basw. co.uk/england/mentoring-scheme/

BASW (2017) Social workers are central to mental health services for children and young people. Available online at: https://www.basw.co.uk/media/news/2017/dec/social-workers-are-central-mental-health-services-children-and-young-people

BASW (2018a) PCF domains rationale for changes (basw_83611-8). Available online at: basw. co.uk, accessed May 2018.

BASW (2018b) *Professional capabilities framework*. Available online at: https://www.basw.co.uk/pcf/capabilities/

Belbin, M (1981) *Management teams: Why they succeed or fail*. London: Heinemann.

Bennis, W (1994) *On becoming a leader*. Reading, MA: Addison-Wesley.

Beresford, P (2011) Radical social work and service users, in Lavalette, M (ed.) *Radical social work today: Social work at the crossroads*. Bristol: Policy Press: 95–114.

Beresford, P (2015) Closing the College of Social Work is yet another attack on the profession. *Guardian*, 23 June. Available online at: https://www.theguardian.com/social-care-network/2015/jun/23/closing-the-college-of-social-work-is-yet-another-attack-on-the-profession

Biestek, F (1963) *The casework relationship*. St Leonard's: Allen and Unwin.

Blackmore, P (1999) Mapping professional expertise: Old tensions revisited. *Teacher Development* 3(1): 19–38.

Bogo, M (2013) Understanding and using supervision in social work, in Parker, J and Doel, M (eds) *Professional Social Work*. London: Learning Matters: 152–70.

Bolden, R, Gosling, J, Marturano, A and Dennison, P (2003) *A review of leadership theory and competency frameworks*. Exeter: Centre for Leadership Studies.

Bowyer, S and Rowe, A (2015) *Social work recruitment and retention*. Dartington: Research in Practice.

Brookes, S and Grint, K (eds) (2010) *The new public leadership challenge*. Basingstoke: Palgrave Macmillan.

Brookfield, S (1987) *Developing critical thinkers: Challenging adults to explore alternative ways of thinking and acting*. San Francisco: Jossey-Bass.

Browning, H, Torain, D and Patterson, T (2011) *Collaborative health care leadership*. Greensboro, NC: Center for Creative Leadership.

Cabinet Office (1999) *Modernising government*. London: The Stationery Office.

Cameron, E and Green, M (2008) *Making sense of leadership*. London: Kogan Page.

Carpenter, J and Webb, C (2012) *Effective supervision in social work and social care*. SCIE Research Briefing 43, London: Social Care Institute for Excellence.

CCETSW (1989) *Rules and requirements for the diploma in social work (paper 30)*. London: CCETSW.

Chatman, J (1991) Matching people and organizations: Selection and socialization in public accounting firms. *Administrative Science Quarterly* 36(3): 459–84.

Children and Young People Now (2016) Chief social worker branded 'spokesperson' for government. Available online at: http://www.cypnow.co.uk/cyp/news/1155683/chief-social-worker-branded-spokesperson-for-government

Clarke, J (ed.) (1993) *A crisis in care? Challenges to social work*. London: Sage/Open University.

Clarke, J and Newman, J (1997) *The managerial state*. London: Sage.

Coffey, M, Dugdill, L and Tattersall, A (2004) Stress in social services: Mental wellbeing, constraints and job satisfaction. *British Journal of Social Work* 34(5): 735–46.

Community Care (2009) Ed Balls: We must make social work a Master's level profession. Available online at: http://www.communitycare.co.uk/2009/03/05/ed-balls-we-must-make-social-work-a-masters-level-profession/

Community Care (2012) Social work membership organisations: Our guide to choosing the right one. Available online at: http://www.communitycare.co.uk/2009/03/05/ed-Social%20work%20membership%20organisations:%20Our%20guide%20to%20choosing%20the%20right%20one

Community Care (2015a) The College of Social Work to close due to lack of funds. Available online at: http://www.communitycare.co.uk/2015/06/18/college-social-work-close-due-lack-funds/

Community Care (2015b) Future of the principal social worker role at risk, says leading PSW. Available online at: http://www.communitycare.co.uk/2015/04/15/future-principal-social-worker-role-risk-says-network-chair/

Community Care (2016a) Hotdesking can add to social worker stress. Available online at: http://www.communitycare.co.uk/2016/08/05/hotdesking-can-add-social-worker-stress-study-finds/

Community Care (2016b) Munro: 'Hotdesking is harming social work'. Available online at: http://www.communitycare.co.uk/2016/04/29/munro-hotdesking-harming-social-work/

Community Care (2017a) Top tips on managing professional boundaries in social work. Available online at: http://www.communitycare.co.uk/2017/06/19/top-tips-managing-professional-boundaries-social-work/

Community Care (2017b) Children's principal social worker role 'has failed spectacularly'. Available online at: http://www.communitycare.co.uk/2017/06/21/childrens-principal-social-worker-role-failed-spectacularly/

Community Care (2017c) Social workers working through illness to keep up with caseloads. Available online at: http://www.communitycare.co.uk/2017/07/17/social-workers-working-illness-keep-caseloads/

Cowden, S and Singh, G (2007) The 'user': Friend, foe or fetish? A critical exploration of user involvement in health and social care. *Critical Social Policy* 27(1): 5–23.

Croisdale-Appleby, D (2014) *Re-visioning social work education: An independent review.* London: Department of Health and Social Care.

Crompton, R (1990) Professions in the current context. *Work, Employment and Society*. Special issue: 147–66.

Crouch, C. (2011) *The strange non-death of neo-liberalism.* Cambridge: Polity.

Cruess, S, Cruess, R and Steinert, Y (2008) Role modelling: Making the most of a powerful teaching strategy. British Medical Journal 336(7646): 718–21.

Currie, G and Lockett, A (2011) Distributing leadership in health and social care: Concertive, conjoint or collective? *International Journal of Management Reviews* 13: 286–300.

Davies, K and Jones, R (eds) (2016) *Skills for social work practice.* Basingstoke: Palgrave.

Davies, K and Ross, J (2016) Skills for leadership, in Davies, K and Jones, R (eds) *Skills for social work practice.* Basingstoke: Palgrave: 162–77.

Davys, A and Beddoe, L (2010) *Best practice in supervision: A guide for the helping professions.* London: Jessica Kingsley.

Department for Children, Schools and Families (2008) *2020 Children's and Young People's Workforce Strategy*. London: DCSF.

Department for Education (2014) *Knowledge and skills statement for approved child and family practitioners*. London: DfE.

Department for Education (2015) *Knowledge and skills statements for practice leaders and practice supervisors*. London: DfE.

Department of Health (1998) *Modernising social services*. Cm 4169. London: Department of Health.

Department of Health (2002) *Requirements for social work training.* London: Department of Health.

Department of Health (2008) *Evaluation of the new social work degree qualification in England.* London: Department of Health.

Department of Health (2015) *Knowledge and skills statement for social workers in adult services.* London: Department of Health.

Diaz, C and Drewery, S (2016) A critical assessment of evidence-based policy and practice in social work. *Journal of Evidence-Informed Social Work* 13(4): 425–31.

Doel, M (2012) *Social work: The basics*. London: Routledge.

du Gay, P (2000) *In praise of bureaucracy: Weber, organisation, ethics.* London: Sage.

Dustin, D (2007) *The McDonaldization of social work*. Aldershot: Ashgate.

Edmonson, D (2013) *Social work practice learning*. London: Sage.

Epstein, RM and Hundert, EM (2002) Defining and assessing professional competence. *Journal of American Medical Association* (JAMA) 287(2): 226–35.

Eraut, M (1994) *Developing professional knowledge and competence*. Oxford: Routledge.

Etzioni, A (1969) *The semi-professions and their organization: Teachers, nurses, social workers*. New York: Free Press.

Evans, L (2008) Professionalism, professionality and the development of education professionals. *British Journal of Educational Studies* 56(1): 20–38.

Evans, T (2010) *Professional discretion in welfare services: Beyond street-level bureaucracy*. London: Routledge.

Evans, T and Harris, J (2004) Street-level bureaucracy, social work and the (exaggerated) death of discretion. *British Journal of Social Work* 34(6): 871–95.

Evetts, J (2003) The sociological analysis of professionalism. *International Sociology* 18(2): 395–415.

Fairtlough, A (2017) *Professional leadership for social workers and educators*. London: Routledge.

Fenge, L and Field, R (2016) Supervision, in Field, R and Brown, K (2nd edn). *Effective leadership, management and supervision in health and social care*. Exeter: Learning Matters: 61–75.

Ferguson, H (2014) Is your social work 'dead' or 'alive'? The gap between inspiring and defensive practice. Harry Ferguson opening speech at JSWEC. Available online at: http://www.communitycare.co.uk/2014/07/23/social-work-dead-alive-difference-inspiring-defensive-practice/

Ferguson, I and Woodward, R (2009) *Radical social work in practice: making a difference*. Bristol: Policy Press.

Field, R and Brown, K (2016) (2nd edn) *Effective Leadership, management and supervision in health and social care*. Exeter: Learning Matters.

Fook, J (2002) *Social Work: Critical theory and practice*. London: Sage.

Forrester, D, Westlake, D, McCann, M, Thurnham, A, Shefer, G, Glynn, G and Killian, M (2013) *Reclaiming social work? An evaluation of systemic units as an approach to delivering children's services*. Bedford: University of Bedfordshire.

Franklin, B and Parton, N (1991) *Social work, the media and public relations*. London: Routledge.

Gambrill, E (2001) Social work: An authority-based profession. *Research on Social Work Practice* 11(2): 166–75.

Gambrill, E and Gibbs, L (2009) *Critical thinking for helping professionals: A skills-based workbook* (3rd edn). Oxford: Oxford University Press.

Gill, R (2012) *Theory and practice of leadership*. London: Sage.

Gioia, D and Chittipeddi, K (1991) Sensemaking and sensegiving in strategic change initiation. *Strategic Management Journal* 12(6): 433–48.

Glasby, J (2005) The future of adult social care: Lessons from previous reforms. *Research Policy and Planning* 23(2): 61–70.

Goodman, S and Trowler, I (eds) (2012) *Social work reclaimed*. London: Jessica Kingsley.

Gould. N and Baldwin, M (eds) (2004) *Social work, critical reflection and the learning organisation.* Aldershot: Ashgate.

GOV.UK (2013) Office of the chief social worker: New appointees start. Available online at: https://www.gov.uk/government/news/office-of-the-chief-social-worker-new-appointees-start

GOV.UK (2015) Social work post-qualifying standards: Knowledge and skills statements. Available online at: https://www.gov.uk/government/publications/knowledge-and-skills-statements-for-child-and-family-social-work

Grant, L and Kinman, G (eds) (2014) *Developing resilience for social work practice*. Basingstoke: Palgrave.

Grint, K (2005) *Leadership: Limits and possibilities*. Basingstoke: Palgrave.

Grint, K (2010) *Leadership: A very short introduction*. Oxford: Oxford University Press.

Gronn, P (2002) Distributed leadership as a unit of analysis. *Leadership Quarterly* 13: 423–51.

GSCC (2005) *Post-qualifying framework for social work education and training*. London: GSCC.

GSCC (2006) *Specialist standards and requirements for post-qualifying framework for social work education and training: Practice education*. London: GSCC.

Guardian (2017a) Children's social care services 'set to reach breaking point'. *The Guardian*, 11 May. Available online at: https://www.theguardian.com/society/2017/may/11/childrens-social-care-services-set-to-reach-breaking-point

Guardian, The (2017b) New alliance gives social work opportunity to take control of its future. *The Guardian*, 19 June. Available online at: https://www.theguardian.com/social-care-network/2017/jun/19/standing-conference-social-work-control-future

Hafford-Letchfield, T, Lambley, S, Spolander, G, Cocker, C and Daly, N (2014) *Inclusive leadership*. Bristol: Policy Press.

Hardcastle, D (2011) *Community practice: Theories and skills for social workers*, (3rd edn). Oxford : Oxford University Press.

Harris, J (2003) *The social work business.* London: Routledge.

Harris, J (2008) State social work: Constructing the present from moments in the past. *British Journal of Social Work* 38(4): 662–79.

Harris, J and White, V (eds) (2009) *Modernising social work*. Bristol: Policy Press.

Harris, J and White, V (2013) *A dictionary of social work and social care*. Oxford: Oxford University Press.

Hartley, J and Bennington, J (2011) *Recent trends in leadership*. London: King's Fund.

Hassard, J and Cox, T (undated) The physical work environment and work-related stress: Mechanisms and consequences. OSHwiki. Available online at: https://oshwiki. eu/wiki/The_physical_work_environment_and_work-related_stress:_mechanisms_and_ consequences

HCPC (2012) *Standards of proficiency: Social workers in England*. London: Health and Care Professions Council.

Healy, K (2005) *Social work theories in context*. Basingstoke: Palgrave.

Higgs, J (2013) Professional socialisation, in Loftus, S, Gerzina, T, Higgs, J, Smith, M and Duffy, E (eds) *Educating health professionals: Becoming a university teacher*. New York: Springer: 83–92.

Higham, P (ed.) (2009) *Post-qualifying social work practice*. London: Sage.

HM Government (2017) *Transforming children and young people's mental health provision: A green paper*, December. Cm 9523. London: The Stationery Office.

Holroyd, J (2015) *Self-leadership and personal resilience in health and social care*. London: Sage.

Holt, J and Lawler, J (2005) Children in Need teams: Service delivery and organisational climate, *Social Work and Social Sciences Review* 12(2): 29–47.

Hood, C and Himaz, R (undated) How does austerity look in retrospect? The UK's recent fiscal squeeze in historical perspective. Available online at: http://blogs.lse.ac.uk/ politicsandpolicy/how-does-austerity-look-in-retrospect/

Horner, N (2012) *What is social work?* (4th edn). London: Sage/Learning Matters.

Howe, D (2008) *The emotionally intelligent social worker*. Basingstoke: Palgrave.

Howe, D (2014) *The compleat social worker*. Basingstoke: Palgrave.

Howe, K and Gray, I (2013) *Effective supervision in social work*. London; Sage.

HSCB (2014) *Coaching and mentoring in social work: A review of the evidence*. Belfast: Health and Social Care Board.

IFS (2017) *The IFS green budget February 2017*. London: Institute for Fiscal Studies.

IFSW (2014) Definition provided by International Federation of Social Workers at the IFSW General Meeting and the IASSW General Assembly. July.

Ingleby, E (2018) *Applied sociology for social work*. London: Sage.

Ingram, R (2013) Emotions, social work practice and supervision: An uneasy alliance? *Journal of Social Work Practice* 27(1): 5–19.

Janis, I (1982) *Psychological studies of policy decisions and fiascos* (2nd edn). Boston: Houghton Mifflin.

Johnson, T (1972) *Professions and power*. Basingstoke: Macmillan.

Jones, R (2009) Children Acts 1948–2008: The drivers for legislative change in England over 60 years. *Journal of Children's Services* 4(4): 39–52.

Jones, R (2015) I've seen the reclaiming social work model cause service implosion. *Community Care*. Available online at: http://www.communitycare.co.uk/2015/04/09/ive-seen-local-authorities-reclaiming-social-work-model-caused-service-implosion/

Jordan, B (2001) *Social work and the third way: Tough love as social policy*. London: Sage.

Jordan, B and Drakeford, M (2012) *Social work and social policy under austerity*. Palgrave: Macmillan.

Kadushin, A and Harkins, D (2003) (4th edn) *Supervision in social work*. New York: Columbia University Press.

Kelley, R (1988) In praise of followers. *Harvard Business Review* 66: 142–8.

Kerno, S (2008) Limitations of communities of practice. *Journal of Leadership and Organizational Studies* 15(1): 69–78.

Kirkpatrick, I (2006) Taking stock of the new managerialism in English social services. *Social Work and Society* 4(1): 14–24.

Knott, C and Scragg, T (eds) (2016) *Reflective practice in social work* (4th edn). Exeter: Learning Matters.

Kolb, D and Fry, R (1974) *Toward an applied theory of experiential learning*. Cambridge, MA: Alfred P. Sloan School of Management.

Kotter, J (1990) *A force for change: How leadership differs from management*. London: Collier Macmillan.

Laird, S (2008) *Anti-oppressive social work: A guide for developing cultural competence*. London: Sage.

Laming, Lord (2003) *The Victoria Climbié inquiry*. London: The Stationery Office.

Laming, Lord (2009) The protection of children in England: A progress report. HC 330. London: The Stationery Office

Langan, M (1993) The rise and fall of social work, in Clarke, J (ed.) *A crisis in care? Challenges to social work*. London: Sage/Open University: 47–66.

Lavalette, M (ed.) (2011) *Radical social work today: Social work at the crossroads*. Bristol: Policy Press.

Lawler, J and Bilson, A (2010) *Social work management and leadership*. London: Routledge.

Le May, A (ed.) (2009) *Communities of practice in health and social care*. Chichester: Wiley-Blackwell.

Levin, E (2004) *Involving service users and carers in social work education*. London: SCIE.

Lipsky, M (1980) *Street-level bureaucracy: dilemmas of the individual in public services*. New York: Russell Sage Foundation.

Lost in Care (2000) *Lost in Care report of the tribunal of inquiry into the abuse of children in care in the former county council areas of Gwynedd and Clwyd since 1974*. London: The Stationery Office.

Lowe, R (2005) *The welfare state in Britain since 1945* (3rd edn). Basingstoke: Palgrave.

Lumby, J (2016) Distributed leadership as fashion or fad. *Management in Education* 30(4): 161–7.

Lymbery, M (2004) Managerialism and care management practice with older people, in Lymbery, M and Butler, S (eds) *Social work ideals and practice realities*. Basingstoke: Macmillan: 157–78.

Lymbery, M (2005) *Social work with older people*. London: Sage.

Lymbery, M and Postle, K (eds) (2007) *Social work: A companion to learning*. London: Sage.

MacDonald, C (2006) *Challenging social work: The institutional context of practice*. Basingstoke: Palgrave.

MacKian, S and Simons, J (eds) (2013) *Leading, managing, caring*. London: Routledge.

MacKian, S, Russell, C and McCalla, L (2013) Preparing to lead, in MacKian, S and Simons, J (eds) *Leading, managing, caring*. London: Routledge: 1–33.

Mantell, A (2013) *Skills for social work practice* (2nd edn). London: Sage/Learning Matters.

Mayer, J and Timms, N (1970) *The client speaks*. London: Routledge and Kegan Paul.

McFadden, P (2015) *Measuring burnout among UK social workers*. Sutton: Community Care.

McGregor, K (2011) Developing leadership among all practitioners. *Community Care*, 22 September. Available online at: http://www.communitycare.co.uk/2011/09/22/developing-leadership-among-all-practitioners/

McKitterick, B (2015) *Self-leadership in social work: Reflections from practice*. Bristol: Policy Press.

Menzies, I (1960) A case-study in the functioning of social systems as a defence against anxiety: A report on a study of the nursing service in a general hospital. *Human Relations* 13: 95–121.

Midwinter, E (1994) *The development of social welfare in Britain*. Buckingham: Open University Press.

Miller, S (2010) A conceptual framework for the professional socialization of social workers. *Journal of Human Behavior in the Social Environment* 20(7): 924–38.

Munro, E (2010a) *The Munro review of child protection: Part one: A systems analysis.* London: Department for Education.

Munro, E (2010b) *The Munro review of child protection: Interim report: The child's journey.* London: Department for Education.

Munro, E (2011) *The Munro review of child protection: Final report: A child-centred system.* Cm 8062. London: Department for Education.

Murray, C and Main, A (2005) Role modelling as a teaching method for student mentors. *Nursing Times* 101(26): 30–3.

Narey, M (2014) *Making the education of social workers consistently effective: Report of Sir Martin Narey's independent review of the education of children's social workers.* London: DfE.

Newman, J (2001) *Modernising governance: New Labour, policy and society.* London: Sage.

Newman, J and Clarke, J (2009) *Publics, politics and power: Remaking the public in public services.* Buckingham: Open University Press.

Northouse, P (2015a) *Introduction to leadership, concepts and practice.* London: Sage.

Northouse, P (2015b) *Leadership: Theory and practice* (6th edn). London: Sage.

Oliver, M and Sapey, B (2006) *Social work with disabled people* (3rd edn). Basingstoke: Palgrave.

Page, R and Silburn, R (1999) *British social welfare in the twentieth century.* Basingstoke: Palgrave.

Parker, J and Bradley, G (2014) *Social work practice* (4th edn). London: Sage/Learning Matters.

Parker, J and Doel, M (eds) (2013) *Professional social work.* London: Learning Matters.

Parsloe, P and Stevenson, O (1978) *Social service teams: The practitioner's view.* London: The Stationery Office.

Pawson, R, Boaz, A, Grayson, L, Long, A and Barnes, C (2003) Types and quality of knowledge in social care. *SCIE Knowledge Review 03.* London: SCIE.

Payne, M (2005) *The origins of social work.* Basingstoke: Macmillan Palgrave.

Payne, M (2006) *What is professional social work?* (2nd edn). Bristol: Policy Press.

Payne, M (2014) *Modern social work theory* (4th edition). Basingstoke: Palgrave Macmillan.

Perlman, H (1957) *Social casework: A problem-solving process.* Chicago: University of Chicago Press.

Pierson, J (2011) *Understanding social work: History and context.* Maidenhead: Open University Press.

Pierson, J and Thomas, M (2002) *Collins Dictionary: Social work* (2nd edn). Glasgow: HarperCollins.

Politis, J (2005) Dispersed leadership predictor of the work environment for creativity and productivity. *European Journal of Innovation Management* 8(2): 182–204.

Pollitt, C (1990) *Managerialism and the public services: The Anglo-American experience*. Cambridge, MA: Basil Blackwell.

Pollitt, C (1993) *Managerialism and the public services*. Oxford: Blackwell.

Pollitt, C (2003) *The essential public manager*. Maidenhead: Open University Press.

Postle, K (2002) Working 'between the idea and the reality': Ambiguities and tensions in care managers' work, *British Journal of Social Work* 32(3): 335–51.

Probst, G and Borzillo, S (2008) Why communities of practice succeed and why they fail. *European Management Journal* 26: 335–47.

Raelin, J (2003) *Creating leaderful organizations: How to bring out leadership in everyone.* San Francisco: Berrett-Koehler.

Reder, P, Duncan, S and Gray, M (2005) *Beyond blame: Child abuse tragedies revisited*. London: Routledge.

Rittel, H and Webber, M (1973) Dilemmas in a general theory of planning. *Policy Sciences* 4: 155–69.

Roe, K (2017) *Leadership: Practice and perspectives* (2nd edn). Oxford: Oxford University Press.

Rogers, C (1961) *On becoming a person.* London: Constable.

Rogowski, S (2010) *Social work: The rise and fall of a profession?* Bristol: Policy Press.

Rogowski, S (2011) Managers, managerialism and social work with children and families: The deformation of a profession? *Practice*, 23(3): 157–67.

Rutter, L and Brown, K (2011) *Critical thinking and professional judgement for social work.* London: Sage.

Satyamurti, C (1981) *Occupational survival*. Oxford: Blackwell.

Schedlitzki, D and Edwards, G (2014) *Studying leadership: Traditional and critical approaches.* London: Sage.

Schön, D (1983) *The reflective practitioner.* London: Temple Smith.

SCIE (2008) *Learning organisations: Key characteristics*. Available online at: https://www.scie.org.uk/publications/learningorgs/key/index.asp

SCIE (2012) *Effective supervision in social work and social care.* Research briefing 43, October. London: SCIE.

Seligman, M (1972) Learned helplessness. *Annual Review of Medicine* 23(1): 407–12.

Senge, P (1990) *The fifth discipline: The art of and practice of the learning organisation.* London: Century Business.

Shaw, I, Jobling, H, Ik Hyun Jang, Czarnecki, S and Ramatowski, A (2016) *The British Journal of Social Work: A case study of applied scholarship, final report 2016.* York: University of York.

Available online at: https://www.york.ac.uk/media/spsw/documents/research-and-publications/History_of_BJSW-2.pdf

Shearer, A (1981) *Disability: Whose handicap?* Oxford: Blackwell.

Shearer, J (2018) Social work leaders must stop hiding and give our profession a voice, *Guardian Social Care Network*. Online at: https://www.theguardian.com/social-care-network/social-life-blog/2018/jan/16/social-work-leaders-must-stop-hiding-and-give-our-profession-a-voice

Sheppard, M (1995) Social work, social science, and practice wisdom. *British Journal of Social Work* 25(3): 265–93.

Singh, G and Cowden, S (2013) The new radical social work professional?, in Parker, J and Doel, M (eds) *Professional social work*. London: Learning Matters: 81–97.

Skills for Care (2006) *Leadership and management: A strategy for the social care workforce*. Leeds: Skills for Care.

Skills for Care (2008) *Leadership and management: A strategy for the social care workforce update 2008*. Leeds: Skills for Care.

Smircich, L and Morgan, G (1982) Leadership: The management of meaning. *Journal of Applied Behavioral Science* 18: 257–73.

Smith, R (2008) *Social work and power*. Basingstoke: Palgrave.

Social Work Reform Board (2010) *Building a safe and confident future: One year on. Detailed proposals from the Social Work Reform Board: December 2010*. London: DfE.

Social Work Task Force (2009) *Building a safe, confident future: The final report of the Social Work Task Force: November 2009*. London: Department for Children, Schools and Families.

Social Worker of the Year Awards (2016) Creative and innovative social work practice. Available online at: http://www.socialworkawards.com/award-entry/previous-winners/2016/yasmin-ishaq/

Stewart, V, Clarke, L and Lishman, J (2009) Leadership and management, in Higham, P (ed.) *Post-qualifying social work practice*. London: Sage: 173–86.

Swain, S and Hillel, M (2010) *Child, nation, race and empire: Child rescue discourse, England, Canada and Australia, 1850–1915*. Manchester: Manchester University Press.

SWAN (2017) What should you know about the new 'national assessment and accreditation system'. Available online at: https://socialworkfuture.org/2017/02/16/what-should-you-know-about-the-new-national-assessment-and-accreditation-system/

Taylor, H, Beckett, C and McKeigue, B (2007) Judgements of Solomon: Anxieties and defences of social workers involved in care proceedings. *Child and Family Social Work* 13: 23–31.

TCSW/BASW (2012) *Practice educator professional standards for social work*. Available online at: https://www.basw.co.uk/resources/tcsw/Practice%20Educator%20Professional%20Standards.pdf

Templeton, R (2016) Improving social work relies on innovative practitioners and service users, not big ideas. Community Care, 20 January. Available online at: http://www.communitycare.co.uk/2016/01/20/improving-social-work-relies-practitioners-service-users-big-ideas/

Thoburn, J, Featherstone, B and Morris, K (2017) The future of social work education in universities is under threat. *Community Care*. Available online at: http://www.communitycare.co.uk/2017/03/07/future-social-work-education-universities-threat/

Thompson, N (2015) *Understanding social work: Preparing for practice* (4th edn). Basingstoke: Macmillan.

Thompson, N (2016) *The professional social worker* (2nd edn). Basingstoke: Palgrave.

TOPSS (2002) *The national occupational standards for social work.* Leeds: TOPSS UK Partnership (training organisation for the personal social services).

Turnbull James, K (2011) *Leadership in context: Lessons from new leadership theory and current leadership development practice.* London: King's Fund.

UNISON (2015) UNISON joins social work campaign. Available online at: https://www.unison.org.uk/news/article/2015/08/unison-joins-social-work-campaign/

UNISON (2016) A day in the life of social work. Research from Community Care and UNISON. London: UNISON/Community Care.

Utting, W (1991) *Children in the public care: A review of residential child care.* London: The Stationery Office.

Waine, B and Henderson, J (2003) Managers, managing and managerialism, in Henderson, J and Atkinson, D (eds) *Managing care in context.* London: Routledge and Open University.

Webb, S (ed.) (2017) *Professional identity and social work.* London: Routledge.

Weick, K (1995) *Sensemaking in organizations.* Thousand Oaks, CA: Sage.

Wenger, E (1998) Communities of practice: Learning, meaning, and identity. Cambridge: Cambridge University Press.

Wenger, E, McDermott, R and Snyder, W (2002) *Cultivating communities of practice: A guide to managing knowledge.* Boston, MA: Harvard Business School Press.

West M, Eckert, R, Steward, K and Pasmore, B (2014) *Developing collective leadership for health care.* London: King's Fund.

White, S (2013) Practising reflexivity: nurturing humane practice, in Parker, J and Doel, M (eds) *Professional social work.* London: Sage/Learning Matters: 39–53.

White, V and Harris, J (2007) Management, in Lymbery, N and Postle, K (eds) *Social work: A companion to learning.* London: Sage: 240–50.

Whittaker, A and Havard, T (2016) Defensive practice as 'fear-based' practice: Social work's open secret? *British Journal of Social Work* 46(5): 1158–74.

Wonnacott, J (2012) *Mastering social work supervision*. London: Jessica Kingsley.

Younghusband, E (1947) *Report on the employment and training of social workers.* London: Carnegie United Kingdom Trust/Constable.

Younghusband, E (1951) *Social work in Britain: A supplementary report on the employment and training of social workers.* Dunfermline: Carnegie United Kingdom Trust.

Younghusband, E (1959) *Social workers in the local authority health and welfare services*, London: Ministry of Health.

Index